Stories from the Road
From the Back Seat

by
Christopher S. Chenault, M.D.

Olympus Story House
www.olympusstoryhouse.com

Table of Contents

Dedication

This book is dedicated to the devoted board of Drive a Senior, Austin, Tx. In addition the many volunteers who have devoted many hours to make sure our clients receive services they need to live at home safely.

Introduction (Preface)

In the early 1980's it became apparent that with changes in Medicare, senior patients began coming home from their hospitalizations needing more help at home than in previous years. In response to this situation a graduate student, Kathy Backus, researched a program in San Antonio where the Robert Wood Johnson Foundation had provided a grant to assist with starting an Interfaith Volunteer Caregiver group. This group of volunteers would provide transportation for these seniors, for medical follow up as well as some evaluation of their care needs.

In 1985, Kathy assisted in forming the West Austin Caregivers, supported by five churches and additional fundraising. That was followed by a similar Caregiver organization in northwest Austin, northcentral Austin, Round Rock and ultimately nine organizations total. These organizations evolved into providing transportation to senior clients who could not drive and other service that included small home handy man services, friendly calls, and activities to help with social contacts. In recent years, in an attempt to clarify our function in our name, we chose to be called Drive a Senior, Austin, Texas.

In 2006, the Beverly Foundation of Pasadena, California published a book, "Stories from the Road." In that book are the stories of volunteer drivers, "who tell about the journey of the volunteer driver: what it's like to meet new people and new challenges; to be an advocate and friend; to take people to life sustaining and life enriching activities; to drive in the local community and spend hours driving to distant appointments; to spend days giving rides to people who need them." The stories are from forty-four organizations across the country that provide volunteer drivers who help people who cannot drive themselves. Generally, the clients are seniors who are taken to medical visits as a priority, but also to the grocery store, the bank and the hairdresser. Clients are also called and checked as to their wellbeing. Games days are held several times each year to provide social interaction between clients.

One of the things frequently mentioned by our volunteer drivers in describing the pleasure of driving these clients is listening to their stories. They have all had long lives and rich experiences that bring joy to the listener. In our new book, "Stories from the Road, from the Back Seat" we have collected a few stories, pretty much at random, from our clients, to give one an idea of the variety of what we hear. Their stories are priceless. You will have to volunteer a number of times to get your own whole story, if that is what you want. Sometimes the last time our clients told part of their story was the last time we drove them to a destination and listened. This listening, we hope, will prevent some of the problems with social isolation for our clients and enrich the lives of our volunteers.

In one of the stories the names are changed at the request of the client.

An Uncertain World
Edgar Haley

Edgar's first memories as a child are those of concrete, molded like bombs along the sides of the streets; a frozen pond behind the house on which the big kids from the neighborhood, both American and German skated; lots of rubble from destroyed buildings with occasional single chimneys standing in solitude in the chaos; a bunker without a roof in which the older kids looked for frogs; and some old crates in the alley that the kids played in and he and his brother used as a hideout. These memories are snap shots of events and places that in later years he cannot be sure are his own. He is not sure if they are of places he remembers or are of images from photographs taken by his amateur photographer father.

He absolutely remembers the smell and taste of the concrete bunker wall on which he rested his arms and chin while he, as a small child, watched the older children, ignore the warning of their parents and wade in the water to look for the frogs. He did not actually lick the concrete, but the smell was so intense it is remembered as a taste. Perhaps it was the mold or deteriorating substance or the mixture of stale water, concrete, and humidity that was so intense.

And it was a mixture of senses that he remembers about the frozen pond. There was the feel of the slippery frozen pond under his feet as he held onto the warm mitten on his mother's hand while walking on the pond along with the icy sense of the cold air and the occasional whiff of smoke from the small fire nearby that was a cacophony of senses to be remembered. In his mind there is a whirlwind of images that pop into place as he thinks back seventy years to his youth. It did not seem strange at the time as it was

1

the only thing that he knew as a child. It is the comparison of the childhood of his later friends that makes it so unique.

Smells have a special place in our minds and his memory is that of the smell riding in the back seat of the car across the long bridge over the rails yard. This was Bremerhaven, a large harbor where fishing boats landed and brought in their loads to be transferred to railroad cars and sent on to the markets inside Germany. Some of the fish did not make it to the rail cars and spilled beside the tracks where they rotted.

The smell was very strong to Edgar and his older brother in the back seat of the car. They would attempt to hold their breath during the long ride on the bridge over the tracks. Pinching their noses helped but they were never able to go the whole distance without having to take a breath and take in the smell. This caused them to giggle and roll around in the back seat which, of course, included taking more big breaths so that their attempt to avoid the smell was thwarted. At least the giggles were fun and a distraction from the bad situation.

The street venders were a warm memory for a child. One man with a wheelbarrow cart that bumped on the rough street so you could hear him coming slowly along would sell balls about the size of soccer balls. They were of different colors and had a distinctive smell of a plastic rubber like substance. He remembers clearly the unique sound they made when bounced on the ground. It was more of a hollow, flat, sound than other balls he remembers. There was little if any real rubber available during and after the War, so they were some sort of synthetic.

Another vender sold hand puppets that were made to look like Punch and Judy dolls, however, in the German tradition of many years the Punch doll was named Karsperl. The heads were carved wood and the rest of the doll make of cloth. The children would plead with their mother to get one. As cash was hard to come by in the early post War years, cigarettes and buttons were sometimes used as a means of exchange.

The family lived in several cities as different assignments took them from place to place. One of the houses had a cherry tree that the neighbor kids would climb much to the consternation of the owner who would chase them away before they could get many cherries. Edgar was not big enough to climb the tree but would get an occasional cherry off the ground.

Edgar started school in Germany attending kindergarten at the age of 5. The school was a community school, conscripted by the American military, to teach the American children as well as the local German children. By the time he entered school he knew a lot of German because of the other children in the neighborhood and because the family had a German maid. He became quite familiar with German by the end of that school year.

The school had its own smell to become engrained in this growing child. In the alley behind the school there were milk bottles discarded in wooden crates without having been washed. The sour milk remained as a fragrant reminder. Much of the milk was concentrated Carnation milk that had been mixed with water as fresh milk was not available.

The family's expedition to Germany was the result of Edgar's father having been assigned there as an active reserve officer in the United States Army. Major Haley grew up in Dallas, the son of a dentist who had started practice in the Oklahoma territory but move to Dallas to start another practice and become a salesman for dental equipment in the area. He joined the reserves in 1938 and then activated in the early 1940's, at the age of 29, when he saw the War coming.

He joined the medical corps and later worked as a medical equipment procurement specialist. He was assigned to Germany in 1946 where the U.S. Army was to set up civilian hospitals as many of the county's hospitals had been destroyed. He was allowed to take his wife, Maryann, and their two small boys, age four and two. And he has arranged for his sister-in-law, a civil servant, to be assigned in Germany as well, so that his wife would not be too lonesome. Major Haley was also an amateur photographer who was always taking pictures in the many locations of his assignments. The houses where they lived were generally commandeered by the military.

Fortunately for the dependents, they were allowed to have a housekeeper for most of their time in country. The first was a German woman, Maria, who did not like the Americans and did not really like working for the family. As there was little work available, she took the job but begrudgingly. She was Edgar's earliest source of the German language. She was obviously unhappy and when things started missing in the house, she was let go.

The second housekeeper was Rhea, who was from Latvia. She and her sister had escaped from their home country when the Russians invaded as the Germans retreated. She was happy to have run from the Russians and was pleasantly employed working for Americans rather than Germans. She was a great source of German in spite of her native Latvian language. Perhaps she was learning German at the same time she was teaching the kids. As time progressed, she met an American GI and, with the help of Major Holey, they were married and obtained papers to move to the States as soon as her new husband had completed his assignment. They moved to California, presumably because that was as far away from Germany as they could get. She sent Christmas cards to the family for over 50 years.

Rhea was quite an energetic person and spent a lot of time with the children. On one occasion she decided to take them to the circus. The problem with that adventure was that the circus was playing in a tent in the Russian zone. They crossed over and back without difficulty, but Edgar's father was quite upset with her, since there were clear risks of being detained on the Russian side. It is assumed that the Russian authorities were simply not interested in children and their babysitter. The Cold War was heating up by this time, as exemplified by the Berlin Air Lift which started with the closing of the roads, trains and barrages into Berlin in June of 1948 and continued until May of 1949.

When stationed in Austria, there was a period when the Russians were more threatening. They apparently had their guns aimed at the hotel where the family was staying, as well as the surrounding city. Major Holey made plans for escape if necessary. The American forces were not stationed locally, so if a Russian attack came, they were told they were pretty much on their own. He packed the car with provision for a hasty departure including a carbine rifle, a .45 pistol, ammunition, bed clothes and blankets, canned goods, and a map. He had gone over a proposed escape route with Maryann as well as several alternative possibilities and had provided a contact in the south of Austria it they needed to go underground. It was about a 150-mile to drive to the Western zone. Maryann had also practiced with the rifle and pistol, so they felt somewhat safer.

Major Holey was a procurement officer in the army. He primarily acquired medical equipment for the hospitals being set up in post-war Germany. As a consequence of his position of procurement officer for medical supplies he made a couple of flights into Berlin during the Air Lift. There were no seats in the plane so on one occasion he sat on canned goods. The intensity and number of aircraft resulted in a plane landing in Berlin every 30 seconds throughout the day and night. Although the Russians never shot at one of the planes, there were some crashes of both American and British planes resulting in the loss of about 100 lives. The assignment was considered rather dangerous.

There were shortages all across Germany and Europe. Many items could not be acquired on the open market. There was a common practice in Berlin, and presumably other communities, in which German citizens would sell their antique furniture in the large market warehouse for points. The points would then be taken over to the American side of the building and exchanged for goods that they needed. In turn, the Americans and British would go to the German side and purchase some of the furniture, china, or crystal being sold. This method was used to control the prices on both sides of the negotiations.

One of the items bought was an air-raid siren. One day Edgar decided to turn the crank to see what would happen. What happened was a very loud noise and his father quickly stopping him, telling him never to do that again. What would the townspeople think? The siren disappeared and he does not remember seeing it again. The family purchased several antique furniture items that they brought back to the States eventually. Edgar clearly remembers going with his mother to a lady's house and bringing home a circular tin, brightly colored with painted flowers, about 3 inches tall, and full of buttons. She treasured that because finding buttons in Germany at the time was basically impossible. Buttons were commonly used as money since there was little cash available. Edgar's mother was quite handy at sewing and would use the buttons.

In addition to her sewing, housework, and other activities, sending letters home each week was a steady ritual. Maryann was from the West Texas town of Iraan. The town was named after the combined first names of Ira and Ann Yates who owned the ranch on which the town was built. The town developed following the discovery of oil on the Yates Oil Field. The towns other claim to fame was the short-term stay in Iraan by V. T. Hamlin, who perhaps created early drafts of his comic strip, Alley Oop, while working in the oil fields.

Maryann continued her task of sending weekly letters home to describe the activities of her husband and family on the boat going over the Atlantic and living in Germany. She was quite detailed in her description of activities and the difficulties of dealing with living in a country that had been almost destroyed in the war. She described the difficulties for the German citizens who had little money and few jobs. A man who was their housekeeper lived with his wife in two rooms with no heat and very little food. She noted that she would have been unable to function if she did not have a German speaking housekeeper and a cook.

And then a sudden change occurred as the family returned to the States for further assignments. Edgar was entered in school in New Orleans during his father's first assignment home. The next year, with a move to San Antonio, he attended the school developed by the military at Fort Sam Houston, followed by North East San Antonio High School. He had developed a real talent for art and so went on to North Texas State in Denton, Texas in 1962. It was an interesting environment, as it was noted for its music, art and photography departments.

The School's distinguishing feature at the time was that it was the only college that provided a degree in Jazz. The art students were noted to be somewhat casual in their dress, partly because of the practical problem of messy paints in the classes. The music students, on the other hand dressed more formally much of the time, with clothes purchased in Dallas. Their dress seemed to have been influenced by their occasional attendance at the symphony and other music events in Dallas and the formal dress they observed there.

Denton had its interesting characters, some more than others. There was a student named Benjamin who was considered quite self-assured and actually quite popular. During his first year he received he draft notice and was celebrated with several parties as he was sent off to defend the country. The next year he was strangely back on campus attending classes. He had somehow managed to be placed in the paper shuffling department that involve the papers for admission and discharge from the army. Things in that department were rather hectic with the number of draftees being processed for the build-up in Vietnam. In the confusion of much paperwork he managed to write his own discharge papers and was separated from the armed services in good standing. He returned to civilian life and never looked back.

At North Texas State, Edgar consolidated a lot of the ideas about art that he had developed along the way. He learned that one line may start at a single point and expand in directions that he had planned, and another might go where he did not. And that is not bad. Even erasing a line can be progress, for it changes the contrast and the depth of the prior lines. And all of those lines will come together to make or break the picture as he has thought of it. Frequently the finished product is much more creative than the original idea and the creation as a whole includes all those fine lines that took on a pattern of their own at times. He thought his art might be a pattern for life and how it may twist and turn in the future.

After two years in Denton, Edgar moved to Austin where he continued his studies in art at the University of Texas at Austin. He thought the art curriculum in Austin rather thin. There was however a lot of information about commercial art in his courses and he found that interesting. He describes the culture in Austin in the mid 1960's as conservative. A person at Barton Springs was beaten up because he had long hair.

So, Edgar fled in a VW van to San Francisco and the San Francisco Art Institute, where he found a comfortable environment on the edge of the down-town ghetto and Japan town, as distinct from China town, where art students could easily dress more causally along with the early hippies. There, several students from Austin and others who attended the art institute, settled in. At the school, modern art was the craze and traditional skills of portrait and landscape painting were little expressed. That experience was not part of Edgar's interest and he lasted a year when the tuition was doubled, and he left for work at the post office and began his efforts to sell some artwork.

The VW van was great for carrying gear and equipment but was not all that reliable mechanically. One of his side art jobs involved painting a billboard white so that it could be re-fitted as a new sign. Well, it was art of a sort, but it paid. That job was north of the San Francisco Bay Bridge and Marin County. On his return trip, he crossed the Bay Bridge and stopped at the toll gate. At that point, the van stopped, and he could not get it running. He cranked the starter many times, to no avail.

With that and the traffic stacking up for a long distance behind him, the bridge personnel had the answer in terms of a large truck with wooden front bumper to push stalled vehicles out of the way. As they were driving the truck into position behind him and about fifteen feet away the van finally caught and started. In a panic, he put it in gear and quickly drove away, with many angry drivers waving arms and other things behind him. He drove to the first off ramp which took him into China town where he drove around for a time hoping no one would come after him.

The van was an adventure on other occasions. At one time, his cable for the accelerator broke and he could not speed up the engine or go anywhere. The motor was in the engine compartment at the back of the vehicle. In his van he had some junk plus a long piece of small rope. This he tied to the lever on the carburetor, lead it out of the engine compartment, down the side of the van and into the driver area. He would then pull on the rope when he wanted to go faster. At one time he held the rope in his mouth, put two hands on the wheel, and leaned forward to pull on the rope to accelerate. He went a week like that until he had it worked on by a mechanic.

Over the years, the character of San Francisco of the late 1960's changed drastically. The anti-war protests, the racial conflict and the drug scene became dominant, affecting everyone's lives. The locals stayed pretty much the same but the outsiders from all areas of the country and even other countries came to San Francisco to be part of "the scene" and the trouble. The ghetto area became much more dangerous, so that getting out at night and even during the day was very uncomfortable for Edgar and his friends.

He began to think about getting out of that complex life and return home. He had met a girl who was a native Californian, and this complicated his decision to return to calm and conservative Texas. The forward progress of his education and artwork were being swallowed up by the conflict around him. His friend, Trader Tom, with his World War I anti-tank gun pointing down the stairwell of their apartment to defend their abode, made him crazy. Yet, San Francisco was such a beautiful city and he loved many of the opportunities there. His girlfriend was not likely to come to Texas which was considered the wild west by many in the big city. He had tried to convince her to come but she was pretty independent and chose not to.

With his mind in conflict, he woke up one morning, gassed up the van and fled to a place where he had felt at home for a time. Maybe he was more suited for the quiet of Texas and the conservative lifestyle. Maybe all those lines on the pages of his artwork were not going where he thought they would and were about to take another direction in his art and life. Even the act of erasing a line in your artwork can be creative for the lost line can send you in a new direction with new contrast. Could he erase San Francisco from his picture and still come out with a whole in the end?

All of his oils and canvases were carefully stowed in the van and he headed out, not for San Antonio where his family lived, but to Austin where his heart called and where he could enroll in the University to gain a master's degree and teach art which was the vocation he had thought of for many years. On arrival, he jumped into the graduate program, but soon found out he did not fit into the current art world and spent much of his time learning about commercial art, design and printing.

He kept in contact with Elizabeth, the girl back in San Francisco, by phone and mail. About six months later she did consent to come to Texas for a visit. Although a small town by comparison she may have found that Austin was greener that she expected and slightly more cosmopolitan. She came for a second visit to San Antonio to meet his parents.

Finally, she made the decision to move to Texas. When she got off the plane, he remembers to this day how vulnerable she looked. And how amazed he was that she had come at all to be with him. She was very independent having been raised by a single mother and having lost her father in the Pacific theater of WWII. She did not have a lot of positive feeling toward her stepfather so that may have played into the decision.

Elizabeth and Edgar moved into a small duplex for a time. When the rent went up as it always does, Edgar had a friend who had an empty cottage behind his house on Comanche Trail at Lake Travis. That was the next stop on the road of many turns.

As luck and providence would have it, Texas Monthly Magazine was founded in 1973 by Mr. Mike Levy and a couple of years later Edgar found a job on the staff. With his knowledge of commercial art, printing, set up and art in general he was a natural for the production department. It was a strange schedule. He worked for two weeks getting the magazine together and to the printer and then had two weeks off. Getting all of the print material in order, selecting pictures, (including sizes), and art to complement the articles, placing ads in various positions through the magazine, incorporating graphics where indicated, placing the follow-up pages of an article later in the magazine, picking the font, creating the table of contents and generally making the presentation of the layout of the magazine attractive were the responsibility of the production department. It was a very busy two weeks but very satisfying for his artistic nature. There was a lot of comradery in the department, so it made for a fun place to work. On his two weeks off he would pick up freelance work for advertisers, most of his business coming from the advertising department of the magazine.

He was successful in having three of his stories published in the magazine. The first was a photo essay and article about Playland Park in San Antonio. This was an amusement park that opened in the 1940's. The next was a story about a Tupperware party he held. He had decided he needed some Tupper ware for his kitchen at home. He had never even considered a party, but then set a date, invited other employees, and opened his apartment for the event. It was a complete success, and the Tupperware sales lady even made some good money. His article about the event was featured in the magazine. His third article was a feature on Historic Old Movie theaters in Texas.

The drawback to the work was the pressure in the two weeks each month working to put all the details of the magazine together.

Then the dam broke. It was as if the line on the page was in a seismograph and recorded a large earthquake, sending the needle to unexpected chaos. One morning he awoke with some decrease in the vision of his left eye. He promptly saw his family doctor who looked at the eye and saw no problem. The next day was somewhat worse and he called his doctor again who referred him to an ophthalmologist. That doctor also saw nothing in the eye.

When the symptoms were worse on the third and fourth day, he called the ophthalmologist again only to find that he was on vacation. The substitute doctor saw him rather promptly and, as the others, saw nothing. He cogitated about the problem and in doing so forgot good communication skills with the patient. Perhaps he was impressed with his own skill of thinking of a rare disorder that no one else had thought of. But he blurted out "I think you may have multiple sclerosis."

With that, Edgar's heart fell to the floor. He was just devastated. He had heard of the disease and asked if he would die from it. The doctor said that was unlikely but there were many unknowns. Magnetic Resonance Imaging was not generally available at that time in the early 1980's, and the finding of multiple sclerosis in the brain were not described yet. There was little to do in the way of treatment at that time. So, he was left to worry, wonder about the future, and make decisions based on little in the way of solid information. It proved to be the crucial event in his life, affecting many decisions and his way of life.

He did have visits with a couple of neurologists who agreed with the diagnosis and who gave him much more information about the disease. They confirmed that this was likely to be a slow process. He would get some element of generalized weakness and fatigue could be a problem. He could have loss of vision in his other eye and other specific functions could be lost. The fact that it most likely would be slow was some relief but he still had many questions that could not be answered and would trouble him from time to time but, how often he did not know. They agreed that the job stress could be a triggering factor.

Edgar talked with his parents and received solid support for his scrambled emotions. They offered to help in any way that they could. He was quite close to his parents and felt their many good qualities would be there for him. One morning there was a knock on the door. His father had driven up from San Antonio to sit and chat.

What he mostly came for was to tell a story. He related the story of a couple of soldiers he had encountered in his dealing with the hospital and his providing medical supplies to various services during his early career. During a training session in the field, these two men were lying in wait for some action. Devastatingly, they managed to get in the way of a tank rumbling across the field. The tank ran over both of them. They survived because they were lying in mud that was sufficiently soft that they were pressed into the ground and not completely flattened. They both had multiple fractures of the legs and pelvis. They were treated for their acute care elsewhere and brought to an Oklahoma facility for their rehabilitation.

On admission, one of the soldiers stated that he was going to fight like hell, and he was going to walk again. The other was very discouraged by his injuries and was much more pessimistic about his chances for recovery. The point that Lieutenant Holey came to tell his son was that the attitude of the two soldiers made all the difference in how they recovered and dealt with their injuries. The one who fought hard and had a good attitude did, in fact, recover rather well in marked contrast to his buddy. Edgar took in what his father was saying. If he approached his illness with a good attitude that would make all the difference. Being a military person of short storytelling qualities, and having completed his mission, his father soon left to drive back to San Antonio. Edgar was left to ponder all of this and to decide how he was going to live the rest of his life with the difficulties he was going to encounter.

Had all of his story lines and all of the drawing lines come to this single point from which all would radiate? Was this part of the drawing even on the page? How could he progress from here to make a complete picture or even *arrange* the pictures on the page?

He would just have to pick up and move along. And he considered his father's story as a gift to his story line that would make a difference in his attitude.

As with all patients diagnosed with multiple sclerosis, Edgar had many unknowns. In what way would he be affected; what areas of function might be lost besides his sight; what will the timing be of this periodic disease; and how rapid might it progress. And how do you live your life with all of these unknowns, which might affect how you can deal with daily activities. He made a crucial decision and left the magazine job where he thought he could no longer complete the tasks with vision only in one eye and where the pressure may have contributed to the onset of the disease. He had a lot of freelance work with still much of it referred from the magazine advertising department.

He entered into a period of strange adjustment. He had not just carried on with his old life but had started a new direction and spent much of the next six to twelve months adjusting to this new approach. He had a number of freelance jobs that mostly came though the advertising department at Texas Monthly and later took a job with the publishing of a travel magazine for an airline. This job also had pressure, as there were articles coming in all the time with no brake as he had experienced before. They published once a week, so the demand was fairly continuous. He even did some work for some small businesses in their advertising needs. Two of those businesses failed so that work was no longer available.

As the opportunities seemed to dwindle in Austin he decided to move to San Antonio where he had other contacts as well as his parents. He father had been promoted to Lieutenant Colonel and Edgar lived with them for a time before moving to an apartment with a friend and then to an apartment that had a month-to-month lease consistent with the needs of military families moving in and out on short notice.

A job came up at San Antonio Monthly Magazine, which was owned by a chain of publishers and lasted for almost two years. He was hired to work in the productions department where his strength lay. He was able to provide some ideas to the production process that did become incorporated into their regimen. But in the end the company was very mechanical in producing the magazine and he was told he was "too artistic" in his approach to putting the magazine together and was let go. Perhaps emblematic of the direction the editors were taking the magazine closed some months later. He moved on to more freelance jobs as well as a job at HEB market, where he found that they were a good organization with which to work. He was on his feet a lot and that was a problem with his generalized weakness.

As his parents were getting older and his father had retired, they wanted to stay active with their respective hobbies. His father had continued to take many photographs and they were entered into art shows around central Texas. His mother painted watercolors and also put her art into shows. Edgar took on the role of driver, taking them around to all of these shows and spending time with them which he found enjoyable. They spent many days driving to the show locations and setting up booths and then spending a quiet weekend talking to people interested in art.

Looming in the background were always the concerns of his continued loss of some vision, occasional tingling in various limbs, fatigue and weakness mixed with the concern about what would happen next and how he would manage to support himself. The vision continued to be a major problem as his left eye remained markedly limited. It became quite clear that this illness, a chronic and relentless phenomenon, disrupted planning in his future. He made a number of changes of direction, jobs, living arrangements, and location as time passed and conditions changed.

Edgar had done some advertising work for Whole Earth Provision Company in San Antonio in the past and used that connection to land a job. This work involved running the toy department. What he remembers most were the Christmas sales rushes, with people everywhere and all talking at once. The most challenging included the post-Christmas returns season. A surprising number of people would return their gifts for a multitude of reasons, mostly because they did not have a use for the item.

This process made him somewhat crazier because of the reverse billing, restocking and being on his feet for long periods. Then in the middle of the Christmas chaos the unthinkable happened. He was waiting on a client when he had a grand mal seizure and fell to the floor. This caused great commotion and a call for an ambulance. He was taken to the hospital where he was evaluated over a couple of days, told it was most likely related to his multiple sclerosis, put on anti-seizure medications, and allowed to return home. This, of course, added shocking instability and worry to his life. The completely unpredictable possibilities of more seizures left him quite distressed. It is one thing to live with a chronic but stable loss of vision in one eye and the periodic numbness that had become almost normal to him. It was another thing to be concerned that at any time he might have another seizure, even with medications. He returned to work at Whole Earth in the same department. It is comical in retrospect, but the lady on whom he was waiting during all of this disturbance kept saying, according to other employees, "Who is going to help me with my return?" "How am I going to get some help here?" Ah, sometimes our focus is so narrow.

He had two more seizures while working in a three-years period at Whole Earth. The Christmas season was always demanding and stressful resulting in increase of his fatigue and concern about progression or flareups of his illness. He left Whole Earth after about three years and moved on.

Another twist in his angular and unpredictable life was to follow. This was a positive event and involved inheriting a small cottage from an aunt, his father's sister, in San Antonio into which he moved. This would provide some respite from his concerns about employment as the cottage was his free and clear.

His parents were now gone, and he was able to furnish the cottage with some of the antiques acquired in Europe during the war. He had grown up with all of those pieces and had a strong connection to them. He lived in that house for about fifteen years but, found that the small jobs that he landed were not keeping up with his expenses. It was difficult to keep the house up to the standards in Alamo Heights as compared to his neighbors. He was now in his mid-sixties and jobs were more difficult to find. Over a period of time, he sold most of his antiques to make ends meet. This was rather crushing as he had lifetime memories with many of these special pieces.

15

It was on a drive to a funeral in Round Rock with friend that he came to the sudden realization that another angle in the lines of his life might be starting to form on the paper. Always these impressions of the form and substance of the picture came in sudden inspirations of how the picture might be put together.

As he crossed Lady Bird Lake in Austin, on their way north to Round Rock, he had a sudden feeling of emotional attachment to Austin as more like home. It was definitely an emotion and not a logical thought. He related to his friends this feeling and they said why not move to Austin, as he still had lots of friends here. Not to mention his old girlfriend. In San Antonio, his housing was difficult to keep up. His driving was more precarious because he had more numbness in his feet and legs. His vision had taken a turn for the worse, and he recognized the emotional attachment to Austin was quite strong. If one has never felt a pull in the chest for a very familiar place or a house, it is difficult to imagine this emotion.

On returning to San Antonio he started the next chapter by putting the cottage on the market. It was in a good neighborhood so he could get a good price and he would no longer have the upkeep problem. The memory of taking a picture of the house with a sold sign in the front yard was a good one so he could think back positively to that step in his journey. He hired a driver to drive his car to Austin because his own driving was limited.

A couple of years later he happened to be in San Antonio and went by the house. As he had expected the cottage was gone and a new house had been built. As he looked at it, he was very pleased with what they had done. The house fit into the neighborhood nicely and the setting was much to his liking. A feeling of satisfaction came to him to replace some emptiness he felt with the loss of his aunt's cottage.

He moved to a place on South Lamar just south of the river but eventually wanted to move to central Austin because his driving continued to deteriorate. At one point he was attempting to back out of a parking place and was burning rubber. He looked down and noted that he had his foot on the brake and accelerator at the same time. Loss of position sense (the ability to tell where your limbs are) is one of the outcomes of multiple sclerosis. Deflated he asked his friend to drive.

He had hand controls placed in his car but never really felt comfortable or safe with that system. On his way home one day, attempting to manipulate the hand controls while going up a hill he came to the realization that driving was somewhat crazy and was no longer appropriate for him. At home he called the KUT (the University of Texas public radio station) vehicle donation number and sighed with relief when the tow truck hauled the car away. He hoped that it would go to someone who could use the hand controls in a more coordinated fashion, and he got a six-hundred-dollar tax deduction.

In addition to his visual problems, seizures, and the loss of sensation in his legs he has had some odd abnormalities difficult to explain. At one point he rather suddenly noted that he was unable to fasten his seat belt. He could grasp the end of the belt and the buckle, but he could not coordinate getting the two together correctly and always had to have help. Then over a short period of time of about 2 years later he noted he was able to perform that maneuver and has continued to do so. At a later time, he found that he could not button his shirts and had to go to pullover type shirts. Again, that lasted a year or two and then resolve. Since both of those activities require bringing the hand across the front or side of the body and getting them together, it seemed apparent that the two problems were related, involving the same area of the brain. Frustrated for a time he was pleased that they resolved.

In Austin he was doing satisfactory with his finances as the had the proceeds from the sale of the house in Alamo Heights. But that was not going to last forever. A lawyer friend suggested that he consider filing for Social Security disability and she could be of help getting through the red tape. What he didn't realize was that for the year after the filing and before any income was available, the rules state than the individual could not generate any income for a year. By this time the cottage money had run very thin and it was frightening to think that while waiting for disability payments he would have almost no income since he was not allowed to work. Just another stumbling place in the road of his unpredictable life.

Through all of this, he has remained rather upbeat and has not let the down turns ruin his life. He has good friends who help look after him. He and a friend walk each day around several blocks. His girlfriend of all these fifty plus years actually pays his rent. Some friends contribute regularly to his income and he gets by. He has had this disease for over forty years, and he has not let it beat him.

His girlfriend fell and broke her arm several years ago and was unable to drive. She got help from Drive a Senior West Austin for the several months when she needed to get to the doctor and grocery store. Drive a Senior, Austin Texas is an organization that through volunteers, provides rides to senior who can't drive as well as other services to help senior stay involved in community and avoid isolation. When Edgar gave up his car, she referred him to this organization and now he has volunteers who take him to the doctor and other necessary trips. Drive a Senior is now a big part of his community.

So, life marches on inexorably and he lives days as they come. He, like the rest of us, don't know what will happen but he seems content and comfortable, if not sometimes anxious about the future. His apartment is neat and organized and has the trappings of an artist without being fancy. And the volunteers of the organization check on him and get him to his appointments. He is surprisingly well adjusted and generally happy.

He describes his recent Thanksgiving and Christmas as very pleasant. He had quiet dinners with Elizabeth and no other company. He walks daily with a friend and neighbor. He is upbeat about life in general and accepts the lingering symptoms. He has a certain calm that is refreshing.

The Magic of Theater

Penny and Gene Young

When the big crash or depression of 1929 came it changed everything. It changed business and home life, street traffic, housing, farming, and it created much despair. But not so much for the Kerr family. Oh, it changed a lot but did not drive them to despair. Grandfather Jewell was the owner of four Studebaker dealerships in Ohio. Since he could not supervise each location, he enlisted his family, including his son-in-law, in the businesses. It was a good living and so they entered into the project with contentment. Then came the crash of the stock market of 1929 and all those businesses were lost in bankruptcy. The sales lots of the company were full of cars bought with borrowed money from the bank and the bank wanted its money. There were no buyers with enough money to buy an automobile and no way to get the money for all of those cars on the lot back to the bank. The banks foreclosed and took the business and the cars. Not that the banks were going to be able to sell them either, but they had some assets that would have some value in the future.

Mr. Jewell senior and his wife had a place to go when their house in Akron, Ohio was lost in the bankruptcy. Mrs. Jewell had a family house in New Hampshire, their former home, that was outside the bankruptcy proceedings, so they move there. Penny's father, Duncan "Mac" Kerr, the son in law, said, "I suppose I should be unhappy about this but I'm not because now I can go back to do what I am trained for."

His training, at Cornell University, was as a metallurgical engineer. He found a job working with the West Vaco Chemical Company with an office in the east San Francisco Bay area of

19

California. California was to be the next stop. Looking for a home Penny's father was rather particular and wanted to live in an active community, perhaps with a university. They chose Palo Alto with Stanford University and eventually bought a house there. That location would require a commute and carpooling across the Dumbarton Bridge in the south bay to the town of Newark on the East side to work. Penny's mother was a Julliard school trained pianist and would teach piano.

Penny Kerr was the youngest of four children and would grow up in the idyllic setting of Palo Alto with Stanford University and its attractions when the town was small and rural. The California weather in that area was mild with seldom any freezing temperature and relatively mild summers in the northern half of the state, moderated by the Pacific Ocean and the lower San Francisco Bay. It is common to have a lot of early morning fog along the coast but the valley in which Palo Alto sits is protected from much of that by the costal range of hills. This was well before the great post-World War II influx of humanity that would sweep away the plum and apricot trees, truck farms and fields covered with grass extending into the hills to the West and to the waters of south San Francisco Bay to the east. The population in 1930 was about 15,000 and grew to 25,00 in 1950 and an amazing 50,000 in 1960.

The house that they bought was quite large with 10 rooms. It had been constructed by the Levi family of the Levi-Strauss blue jean company. Many of the homes in the area were of Mediterranean style with white stucco walls, tile roofs and terrazzo walkways.

During the Second World War, with all the young men drafted into the conflict, there were insufficient laborers to pick the crops of plums. At one point it was anticipated that the rainy season was coming, and the crops needed to be picked or they would be ruined by the rains. As a consequence, the farmers came to the junior high school and asked for volunteers to help pick the fruit. Penny became one of those volunteers and, with other student volunteers, was taken by bus to some groves where they spent the morning picking plums and placing the fruit in field boxes to be taken to the packing houses. What a fun and different way to get out of school for a while.

The nearby community center became the focal point of Penny's young life. This creation was provided by a benefactor named Lucie Stern. Apparently, the Sterns had a daughter born with a significant disability which led the family to give to the community this activity center in her memory. In this project there was space for parties, dance and music classes, craft rooms, adult and children's theater, Boy and Girl Scout rooms, swimming pools, tennis courts, and instructors on full time staff to teach these activities. There was even a "secret garden" between the children's theater and the children's library.

Penny remembers growing up spending hours in the theater area and was in her first play at age three playing the part of a pansy. Her distinguished line was, "I am a pansy." That was followed by participating in many plays and acting classes. There was a woman instructor who would use the stories in some of the books of the library to create plays for the children. They had a full-time set director and an amazing support staff.

At the center of the complex, there was a large courtyard with open space to play. A May day celebration was created each year with 6-8 fully decorated May poles with tapes that the children would use to weave and cover the poles. There was an annual pet parade with local area organizations manning booths for refreshments to sell as fundraisers.

If Penny wanted something else to do as she got older, she could ride her bike over to Stanford and go to the museum, the theater or the Sanford Lake. She attended school at the Palo Alto, Walter Hayes Elementary School and then the David Star Jordan Jr. High School that was new and had 900 students attending from all over the city and surrounding area. One thing that impressed her was the large bicycle shed that provided room for at least half of the children's bikes, as many rode to school.

December 7, 1941 remains surprisingly clear in her mind as it does for many. She was staying overnight with a friend, Patsey McKaye. That morning Mr. McKaye was sitting in the living room reading the Sunday paper and listening to the radio as the kids were on the floor playing a game. The commentator on the radio broadcast reported the news of the bombing of Pearl Harbor. Her immediate reaction was concern because she had an uncle who worked at Pearl Harbor. Fortunately, it was Sunday and he was not on the job that day. He actually did not live in Honolulu but "over the poly" as they say in the Islands. He lived on the other side of a mountain in a quieter side of Oahu.

Palo Alto was typical in many ways of the California of that time. Kids played outside until it was dark or dinner time. Everyone trusted their neighbors and doors were seldom locked. The children rode their bikes everywhere as traffic was not of much concern. One evening the gang of girls decided to camp out. They chose the backyard orchard of a friend in the group as the place to spend the night.

The next morning the girls, then about age 12, decided to ride their bikes across town to a friend's house. When they arrived, their friend's mother asked if they had told their parents where they were going. They had not. So, they were lined up at the phone on the wall to call their parents, let them know where they were, and say, "we are staying for lunch."

There was a unique opportunity in the community during the war. As there were a large number of servicemen stationed in the area, families could sign up to host them for dinner on Sundays. Penny's family entered into this custom and would have two or three men at a time for dinner. On a couple of occasions, the family would serve artichokes as an appetizer. They would play a game on the visitors by sitting quietly without eating to see how they would deal with eating the artichokes. Finally, all would laugh, and the green horns would be shown how to peel off the leaves from the head, dip them in mayonnaise and strip the succulent part of the leaf off with their teeth. The meal would frequently involve cooking a large turkey as turkeys were not rationed. It was quite entertaining to have the visitors from all areas of the country and to hear stories involving their home states, especially with the different accents.

She was twelve in 1942 when the family moved to Carmel when her father took a job with Kaiser Industries to become the general manager of Kaiser's three plants in the area. That was a move from one ideal community to another. Carmel was the storied beach town on the west coast south of San Francisco at Monterey Peninsula and was the setting for John Steinbeck's book "Cannery Row" written only three years after the family moved to the community.

Carmel sits between coastal hills and the ocean on a point of land that is the lower prominence of the California coast that forms a huge bay, Carmel Bay. The bay is known for the appearance of humpback and blue whales as well as Orcas and Dolphins that feed in the rich waters of that area in the summer and fall. Families will take picnics to the rocky shores to sit and watch by the hour as the huge animals play and broach the placid waters of that area. Many an artist has sat on the coast to watch and paint the grandeur of the scene. In addition to the attractions of the sea, the area is dotted with cypress, pine and oak trees. The cypress trees are perhaps the most noteworthy as they often jut from rocky out-croppings along the shore and take strange and distorted shapes because of the strong costal winds.

Mr. Kerr was to work at Kaiser, a huge steel and metallurgical business that was also involved in trying to take minerals out of sea water. Mr. Kerr was to become the world authority on heavy media separation, namely the separation of elements from sea water. Aluminum was in particular demand and was to be used in building victory ships by Kaiser. The Kaiser company had been recruited to manufacture as many ships as possible during World War II, mostly for troop transport.

Penny's mother stated that the house they bought in Carmel was a "bird house" compared to their ten-room house in Palo Alto. Beach houses in the early years of California were quite modest in size as they were more beach cottages for vacations or the small homes of people who were outside the economic mainstream but living their dream close to the ocean and surf. And there was the colony of artists with pallet in hand out to paint the next museum piece.

Penny started high school in Carmel. One of her best memories of that time was that for the first time she was known as Penny Kerr and not as the younger sister of her brother, Duncan, or sisters, Charlotte and Peggy. Of course, the beach at Carmel was wonderful if not somewhat chilly. The children walked everywhere as there was little gasoline available during the war. By stretching the truth at age 15 she got a job working in the restaurant in a hotel where the pay included two meals the days she worked. That meant her family did not use sugar, butter and meat for her meals when she ate there. That excess of rationed food allowed her mother to use the extra sugar to can fruit.

The job allowed Penny to purchase Victory Bonds that were considered a patriotic duty. The area around Carmel and Monterey was covered with truck farms where strawberries and many varieties of vegetables, mostly lettuce, were grown. Mr. Kerr was a member of the Rotary club and there was a lot of exchanging of produce among the members.

Working for Kaiser, Mr. Kerr was assigned a work vehicle that was a pickup truck. That transportation allowed Penny to get a job at a theater in town at the Carmel Playhouse, where she was an usher and served coffee. Her father could pick her up at night after work. Carmel during the war was very dark at night as houses were required to have blackout curtains and there were no city streetlights. Cars were not allowed to run with headlight on and had to use their parking lights.

On one occasion, while driving home, her father stopped and had her get out with a flashlight and illuminate a tree that he knew was in the roadway, so they could avoid running into it. There were many large pine and evergreen trees in the community. Carmel was close to Fort Ord and the coast, so the precautions were felt necessary to prevent the enemy from targeting the fort. Carmel had been mostly an artist's colony before the war but, during the conflict, became an officer's colony for those stationed at nearby Fort Ord, a little way up the coast. During and shortly after the war the town and school grew such that the1946 graduating class was the largest ever at 60 students.

While in high school there was no theater group or instruction in dance as the school was so small. There was a gymnasium in which they held sock hops from time to time. The music for these dances were provided by boys in the school that had record collections and who became the disc jockeys for the events. For more formal dances, such as Valentine's day dances, they had bands from the local community, and they were held in the cafetorium.

Some exciting entertainment was on occasion provided by a couple of boys who would play boogie-woogie side by side on the piano. They had diverse backgrounds with one from an upper-class family and the other the son of the local police chief. The music brought them together as good friends.

Following high school, Penny attended The University of California at Berkley majoring in theater arts. She sang in the university chorus and was thrilled at one point when they performed Beethoven's 9th accompanied by the San Francisco Symphony. Her family made many trips to Berkley to view her productions especially the opening night events. During that period, she was lucky to have an instructor in dance named Madam Kosloff who, with her husband, had their main studio in Hollywood.

One summer, while a student at Berkley, she was taking a class and decided to volunteer as a helper within the theater department. When she asked what she could do to help, she was taken on to "hold the book." She had no idea what that meant. She was told that she was to hold the book of the script of the play during rehearsals and when someone missed a line, she would prompt them.

One day she was asked to go on stage and stand in for the lead role as the student who had the part was absent. The instructor told her that the cast would assister her in moving around the stage so she could be in the correct position to read her lines. With book in hand, she went through the rehearsal reading her part as instructed. At the end of the rehearsal the director said, "You read the part so well. Do you want to take on the role?" She responded that she was taking summer school classes. He responded emphatically, "Well drop them." She dropped the classes, took the role, and the show went on. It was her first leading role in a play. With that experience being so positive she became a Theater major. She is not sure what happened to the student who had the lead role in the first place. Overall, she had a very positive experience in theater and dance at Berkley,

Following graduation from Berkley, the family discussed whether Penny would best go to Hollywood where she knew the Kosloffs or whether she would try New York. Her family thought Hollywood was rather risky and less suitable. Her mother had studied at the

Julliard School making that an attractive alternative. It was a world leader in music and had just added dance. The Kerrs had extended family on the east coast. It would be a fabulous opportunity if she could get into Julliard, but an audition was necessary for

She arrived in New York City two weeks before her scheduled audition and stayed with a cousin in New Jersey. She also had a friend in New York who had been a student at Berkley while Penny attended. Not surprisingly a number of theater student move to New York for the opportunities. As part of a city tour provided by her cousin, they visited Columbia University campus. The university is located on 116th street in Manhattan not far from Julliard on 124th Street. In the line at the registrar's office to get his G.I Bill payment was another friend of a friend by the name of Gene Young and they were introduced.

Penny had applied to Julliard as a dance major. Her audition day arrived, and she sat nervously in the wings of the school theater as other students were interviewed and asked to present their prepared dance routines. As she sat in the wings, she could hear the comments of the faculty who were sitting in judgement of the various presentations. The student before her was either not a strong dancer or not well prepared and the faculty was shredding her performance with their comments. This made Penny even more nervous.

Their audition presentations included two elements. The first was a piece that the student had prepared beforehand and had practiced well before the event. In the second part the faculty provided the student with a verbal list of moves that were to be performed based on the order of moves on the list. Her first presentation went satisfactorily but when presented with the list of moves to be made Penny stood still and silent for a long moment. The faculty asked if there was something wrong. Penny's response was that her longtime instructor in California was Madam Boldina Kosloff, who had always provided instructions in Russian. The list presented to Penny was in French, terms she had never heard before. None of the terms were even the slightest familiar to her. Fortunately, there was a faculty member present who could translate and so spoke in Russian the twenty moves and positions to be performed so Penny could complete her audition. The audition went quite well and she was admitted to Julliard for her studies. Her family was very proud of her as Julliard school is highly competitive as one of the most prestigious conservatories in the world with a student acceptance rate of around six to eight percent.

Although her audition was with dance performance, she completed a year at Julliard with a certificate in dance notation, the practice of placing on paper the symbols for the dance moves performed by the dancer, like music notes on a paper. Her long-range interest was in production of performances where dance was incorporated in the theatrical event and produced for children. This skill would provide her the tools to outline on paper the moves to be performed on stage.

She was following in the footsteps of the instructor in Palo Alto who had created plays for children from children's books in the library. This talent had been reinforced in her studies at Berkley when she produced a student play based on a Czechoslovakian fairy tale in pantomime. In that project she had to create her own set pieces and lights because most of the sets and props in the theater department were being use by the department chairman for a production of Hamlet.

Her student crew created a large book as a set on the stage where the pages would be turned by the reader as the story unfolded. She used parachute material dyed green for some of the backdrops. A little girl reader sat on a raised platform on the side of the stage and read the story as others acted out the parts. True to her leaning she included some dance in the story. She had a lot of fun choosing music for the production. After listening to a number of selections, she settled on a piece by Mozart recorded at 78 rpm speed but played at 33 rpm to try for a fantasy mood. And it worked.

Apparently, the production was considered very good by the faculty and other students. The chairman of the department said to the students at the first class, "You, "A" students might as well be warned that I don't give "A's" in my classes" True to form Penny got a "B" for the production assignment and she had expected no more.

Gene Young was born in Hazzard, Kentucky but moved quite early with his family to near-by Lexington. His father was a business entrepreneur as well as a pilot. On moving to Lexington, Mr. Young purchased a bakery that became quite profitable and he expanded that including five bakeries. He purchased some land near Lexington and soon built the first airport in town.

From a very young age, Gene wanted to learn to fly. He ordered magazines with many airplane related issues and constructed a number of model airplanes. His father would try to get hold of the magazines so he could read them first so there was a little friendly competition between them. He taught Gene to fly in his early teens. Upon graduation from high school at age 16, he enrolled at Saint Louis University Air Parks College (later to include aircraft Engineering, Aviation, and Technology). This was the first federally certified school of aviation in the country. It was located in east Saint Louis where there is a long history of aviation firsts.

While in school his father would fly over from Kentucky to take him home for holidays. He had graduated from high school in 1943 and was seventeen during his year at Parks College. In the spring of 1944, the World War II was raging and he decided to sign up for the Navy air corps. They told him it would be some time before his name would come up for enlisting since he was only seventeen.

In June he turned eighteen and shortly thereafter the Navy called to offer him a chance to enlist. After enlistment he was sent to Duke University for college studies in mathematics, aeronautics, and astronomy for navigation. By the time that was completed, fortunately for him the war was over. He asked for and was assigned to multi-engine aircraft. He was sent to San Diego and Florida for flight training. Of course, they had to learn to land at an airstrip but also to land on an aircraft carrier.

Pan American Airlines, founded in 1927, was flying across the country and was also flying to South America. Gene decided he wanted to fly multi-engine airplanes and be the youngest pilot to fly the route to South America. Pan Am was interested in long range flights and had talked about flying across the Pacific. No airplane before World War II could fly that distance. The airline had explored various potential routes and sent technicians to Hawaii, Wake island,

Guam, Japan, China and other locations to look at possible airports well before the war and the Japanese invasion of these same islands.

Gene was assigned to the Pacific and was flying freight and some personnel all around the Pacific after the War. He had the good fortune to fly to all of the islands Pan Am had looked at years before, although not on a commercial airline but with the Navy. He was not involved in any combat. He had experienced much of what he had wished for in earlier years but experienced these long flights in the navy and not with Pan Am.

In June of 1948 the Berlin Airlift was started as a way of supplying that city with all the goods necessary to keep the city alive when the Russians blocked the roads, canals, and rail traffic across the Russian sector of East Germany. Germany had been divided into four sections administered by Russia, France, Great Britain, and the United States. Russia closed off access to Berlin over a dispute about money, namely the introduction of the Deutsche Mark in the western section. The Army was doing the flying and delivering everything from coal to water, food, and other supplies and was having a lot of crashes or near crashed at night and in bad weather. The Navy command said they could help as the Navy pilots were well versed in instrument flying in bad weather and at night. A number of Navy pilots including Gene's squad were then assigned to Frankfurt, Germany. At the time Gene was 22 years old and one of the youngest pilots flying the airlift.

Over the next year of the airlift he flew 40 missions into and out of Berlin on a hellish schedule. He would take off from the airport in Frankfurt and land in Berlin at one of two airports, Tempelhof or Gatow. The planes were on a schedule that had a plane landing in Berlin every thirty seconds. The planes were quickly moved to hangers or tarmacs where they were unloaded. The pilots had enough time to almost drink a cup of coffee, jump back into their planes and be off again.

Adding to the stress and tension of the flight schedule was the harassment of the planes by Russian jets that flew on either side of the flight path as they flew the 100 miles back and forth from Berlin to the Western zone. Although the Russians never fired at one of the transport planes, it was nerve wracking to have them practically right on their wing tips the whole time. It was always hard to tell if that portion of the cold war would heat up at any time. The pilots' schedules would allow them to have a day off between shifts. On one occasion Gene was not feeling well and went in for a medical check-up. The doctor told him that he was fine and just needed a rest so suggested he take a couple of days off, one more than his usual one day.

The Russians relented by ending their blockade in May of 1949 and opened the roads, canals, and railroads. The Airlift was terminated after a couple of months when the western nations of Britain, France, and the U.S. were reasonably certain the Russians would not close things down again. The flights were stopped in September of 1949. They had made some 278,228 flights and delivered almost two million tons of food.

In the hectic schedule of flights and rotating personnel, although Major Haley, the father of Edgar Haley, (from our previous story) made three or four of those flights with his medical supplies. We will never know if he flew on any of Gene Young's flights. With the end of that Cold War tactic the Navy pilots were assigned back in the States. Gene completed his five-year enlistment in 1950 and decided to leave the world of flying. He said that flying those planes was a lot like being a glorified bus driver, although with more hair-raising situations. He had wanted to fly from a very early age, be the youngest pilot around, flying the long routes over the South America and the Pacific he had dreamed about, and he had completed that experience. That was enough. Following his retirement, he never piloted a plane again in his life and, oddly, had no desire to do so.

A complete about-face was in order. From his early and eager interest in flying he chose a very different direction. He had some college credits from Duke University completed during his basic training in the Navy. The GI bill allowed him to attend Columbia University in New York with a major in Comparative literature as an undergraduate. The G.I. Bill was a wonderful earned gift to returning veterans. Gene followed his undergraduate years by undertaking a Master's degree, also in literature. Penny and Gene had met while Gene was working on his masters and in line to collect his GI bill payments.

Penny finished Julliard in 1952 and in 1953 they traveled to California to be married under the close supervision of Penny's mother and father. Thus, Penny Kerr became Penny Young. Gene was scandalized by the limited reading Penny had done almost exclusively related to theater and dance so, provided her with a reading list shortly after their marriage.

Following completion of their studies in New York, Gene applied for and received an appointment to the faculty of the University of Kentucky in Lexington, his former hometown. On arriving in Lexington, Penny found it to be a beautiful community with a surrounding area including many colonial houses, beautiful horse farms, lovely white fences, green pastures, and large trees.

As a prelude to future events, Gene's mother decided to have a party to introduce Penny to her friends in the community. Strangely, the party turned out to be a bridge party and Penny did not play bridge. As a consequence, she served coffee and cookies to the guests and did not have a lot of opportunity to visit with the ladies. She came to realize with time that this social structure in the South was not welcoming if you were not born in the area.

Another detraction to the community was the strong smell of tobacco being dried in the barns in the fall that permeated the community. If you did not like the smell it was hard to get used to. Penny became the Geology Department librarian at the university as she felt quite at home in libraries because she had spent much of her young life in the library in Palo Alto. The fact that her father also had a background in geology allowed her some familiarity with the language. She had also taken a number of Geology courses at Berkley.

After two years, Penny was rather fed up with Lexington's closed culture and decided she would leave Lexington with or without Gene. So, without prospects they moved to Berkley, California. Penny found a job in the rare book section of the library at the University of California which felt like home. One of the conditions of her employment was that she had to be in the room with any visitor wanting to use any rare book. They were only allowed to read in one specific room of the library. Since she had to be present at all times she asked for and was allowed to read any of the books she chose. As a consequence, she was able to read first editions of Mark Twain, Shakespeare, and many other writers.

Gene, looking for job possibilities in literature, visited the Theater department at the University of California, Berkley. He was interviewed by the chairman of the department where Penny had been a student, six years earlier, when she created her play involving the use of the Czechoslovakian fairy tale. Gene stated he was married to Penny Kerr and asked if the professor remembered Penny as one of his students. He responded that he certainly remembered her as the "creator of the best student production we have ever had in the department." And it only got a "B."

Gene eventually accepted a job teaching English to students at the Armstrong Business College. Among the many students, there were a number of foreign students who had no experience reading English literature. They had no cultural background in the likes of Mark Twain, Steinbeck, Conrad, or Hawthorne and this gap made for a lot of stumbling trying to relate the English language to these students. Many English idioms include references to characters in our history with whom they had not the least familiarity. This required an explanation of the reasoning behind each idiom and many phrases in English. In 1957 he applied for and was accepted into the Stanford Theater PhD program. He completed all of his required studies but never completed his dissertation to obtain the degree.

The year after he started the program, they had a son, Christopher (Kit) who complicated their time schedule. In 1960, a position became available, and Gene accepted a job in the speech department of Fordham, the Jesuit college, (later to become Fordham University) in New York City. This allowed them to return to New York where they would both feel at home near the colleges they had attended. And they both loved the theater, so opportunities would abound. They moved to New Jersey right across the river from New York in the town of Rutherford.

Rather than living in busy and expensive New Your City they decided to live in New Jersey and Gene would commute to work. Penny's mother had a cousin who was a lawyer also living in New Jersey. He assigned one of his secretaries the job of looking around the state for a suitable community in which to live. They suggested Rutherford for its location and its schools as suitable place. The town was close to the tunnel under the Hudson and Gene could take the bus right into town and walked a short distance to Fordham College.

One very significant factor to be considered in the decision to move to New York and away from California was the promise that Fordham College was invited by the Lincoln Center Renewal Project to be part of the new Performing arts complex. The Complex would become the Lincoln Center for the Performing Arts, future home of the Metropolitan Opera and the New York City Ballet. There was talk of breaking ground in 1964 but that did not happen until 1966.

His position allowed him to development the Theater Department in that project. Close to the time when construction began the person who had hired him at the Fordham College died. Gene became the acting chair of the Speech and Theater department. That department would later become the Fine Arts Department. In his position he was heavily involved in increasing the number of theater students and was a principle in teaching theater students all areas of theater including the business of running a theatre.

In addition, there were courses in directing, acting, play writing, and the history of theatre. Some of the schools more famous students were Denzel Washington, Alan Alda, Geraldine Ferraro, G. Gordon Liddy, Andrew Mark and Chris Cuomo, David Copperfield, Donald Trump, and Vin Scully, the sports caster. They also taught Mike Able who later became a council man in New York City. Gene was credited with developing the curriculum for the theater department and increasing the number of plays presented at the Lincoln Center. Gene was very interested and well-read in history and therefore, when teaching theater and speech, he would include the history of that particular period. That proved to be very popular with the students. Many of them kept in contact with him even after his retirement and the move to Texas.

Meanwhile, Penny worked part time at the public library, taught dance and acting in private lessons, worked in a real estate office for a time, and raised their sons, Kit, who later became a multimedia visual artist and Ted, who would become an architect. She was on the school board for 9 years, including two years as president.

After several years living in Rutherford, that had had a great school system, they became disillusioned with the community. Support for the school system became poor as the lack of school bonds passages dwindled. They just wouldn't spend the money necessary to provide adequate room for the children of a growing community. The school system started running split school sessions that were highly inconvenient for the families.

Four families, all friends very interested in the school system, searched New Jersey for a better school system. Penny's family found Tenafly after much looking. Eventually all four families moved to that city, a little further north but still across the Hudson River from NYC.

Through all of this, they lived in these very nice communities and had a playground of activities in New York City with museums, musicals, chamber music, plays, restaurants, and all the glitter of the Great White Way. Upon his retirement, Gene was honored by the City of New York for his development of theater at the Lincoln Center and the school of fine arts at Fordham University. Penny, with her many interests, never achieved the goal she had in her early life of developing children's books into plays for children. She was active with many pursuits including the local library, teaching dance, much work with the school board, real estate, heavy involvement in the local garden society and raising two successful sons. Penny had a friend of a friend who was the principle Oboist of the ballet orchestra. That provided the opportunity to acquire low cost tickets to the dress rehearsal performances. Over the years she was able to see the entire repertoire of the New York Ballet.

Following retirement Gene became more involved with the New Jersey Cactus and Succulent Society, became the president and, as an avid reader, became an expert about those plants and lectured around the state at garden clubs.

Gene started writing a book in partnership with a friend discussing the influence of philosophy at different periods of history and its influence on theatre. Unfortunately, his friend died suddenly and the energy to complete the book was lost, so was never finished.

In 2004, they were encouraged by son, Ted, to move to Texas when he stated that their granddaughter needed grandparents close by. Ted wound up in Texas because he came to the University of Texas for a specific and special Master's program in architecture and was later offered a job in Austin that was too good to turn down. His wife, an architect as well, had opportunities in her own right. With Penny and Gene's move to Austin, they eagerly joined the Austin Symphony, Austin Ballet, and theater programs. With their background in New York level entertainment they were spoiled and found they liked some of the programs here better than others. From some they withdrew but remained entertained by their granddaughter's activities. She is now grown and off to college in Cincinnati with plans to be an interior designer that, interestingly, combines the artful element from one artist uncle and elements of architecture and design from her father and mother.

In the last chapter, as age crept upon them, Gene's eyesight failed him for driving and then he passed away at age 93. Penny remains alert and active at 92 but slowed down by bad knees and is hesitant to continue driving. She was introduced to the Drive a Senior organization to be part of her community and to help with transportation when her family is not available. She lives in the home she shared with Gene and has a housekeeper most days. She is content in life with her bougainvilleas on the back porch, puzzles in the living room, much reading, and a comfortable home in which to live.

As a final chapter, her son, Kit, is moving his multimedia art practice to Connecticut, although he is getting close to retirement. Son, Ted, has bought an older house in New Your, north of the city, that he and his wife, as architects, will remodel. Ted's daughter has attended the University of Cincinnati and completed her studies in interior design and is scheduled for an opportunity in New York. Penny will leave Austin and return to her stomping grounds near New Your City and the entertainment she so enjoys, with her family close by.

Palo Alto, Carmel, Berkley, Julliard in New York, Lexington, Kentucky, short return to California, move to New York with a life filled with the theater, raise two talented children with a very compatible and interesting husband for sixty plus years, spend 20 years in Austin, Texas and will spend her final years back in New York with family. Can it get better than that?

Blind Travelers in this World

Ann and Douglas Foxworth

Rubella, also known as German measles, was once a common childhood illness, generally mild and unrelated to standard measles. However, it can infect unvaccinated adults. A major U.S. outbreak in 1964-65 saw 12.5 million cases. Rubella is particularly dangerous for pregnant women, potentially causing infant death, deafness, blindness, intellectual disability, or a combination of these symptoms known as Rubella syndrome.

In 1944, Marcia Foxworth, living in Pasadena, Texas, became pregnant with her fourth child, having never contracted rubella as a child. At that time, an effective vaccine was not yet available—it wouldn't be until 1969. During her pregnancy, she contracted the rubella virus, at a time when the dangers of rubella during pregnancy were not well understood.

In 1941, following a large epidemic in Australia the previous year, an eye physician observed 68 cases of congenital cataracts in infants born to mothers who had contracted rubella early in their pregnancy. He also noted other issues in these infants, including hearing loss, intellectual disabilities, and congenital heart disease.

Unfortunately for the Foxworth family, information about rubella syndrome had not been widely disseminated to the medical community by 1944, so no issues were noted at birth. With three healthy older children and another born without problems in 1947, there was no suspicion of any concerns.

Around his first year, it became clear that Douglas Foxworth wasn't making eye contact or smiling back at people. It was noticed that while he would play with a toy or ball if it was right next to him, he showed no interest if it rolled away. Unlike his siblings, who appeared to develop normally, Douglas's behavior stood out. His father, a shift worker with irregular hours, often slept during the day and had limited interaction with the children. Additionally, his father's reluctance to acknowledge the possibility of a disability delayed early recognition of Douglas's condition.

Douglas doesn't recall much effort at home to help him with tasks that were difficult, as his family lacked the knowledge for such creative teaching. He doesn't remember when it was determined that he was mostly blind, though his cataracts were likely visible to his doctor. One memory that stands out is a game his father played with him, where he would place different denominations of paper money in front of Douglas and ask him to identify them. If he got them right, he was promised a dollar, but even when he didn't, his father still gave him a dollar. Douglas also doesn't recall his mother helping him much with dressing; he managed that on his own just like all the other children.

Douglas' siblings often played outside while he mostly stayed indoors. Rather than feeling lonely, he felt safer inside, surrounded by his toys, familiar surroundings, and close to his parents. Though his vision allowed him to see some shapes and shadows, it was enough for him to learn to ride a bicycle, which gave him a sense of freedom and independence. He enjoyed playing with the water hose, often squirting himself and occasionally his siblings if they got too close. However, he was excluded from games like hopscotch and "Jacks," which his sisters and their friends played, leaving him isolated from the visual world and from potential playmates.

From an early age, Douglas developed a keen interest in electricity and electronics. He would unplug the toaster from under the breakfast table, much to his parents' dismay, but he knew not to touch the metal prongs. He built imaginary circuits using a cardboard box, a pull-chain switch, and light bulbs. This early fascination grew, and later he would visit electronics and radio shops in Pasadena, where he learned how to safely deactivate a 16,000-volt capacitor in a TV set and replace the main tube. His tinkering made him quite dexterous, a skill that would prove valuable in the future.

Besides his interest in electronics, Douglas was thrilled when he received a 33 ⅓ speed "talking book" recorder, which he listened to frequently. This system, part of a Texas program that began in 1918 with an appropriation for raised letter books in the State Library, eventually included recorded books that enriched his world and fueled his imagination.

Douglas also had a deep love for music. In the evenings in Pasadena, Texas, near Houston, he and his parents would tune into distant radio stations from places like Tulsa, Oklahoma, and Fort Worth, Texas. On good nights, they could even catch the Grand Ole Opry from Nashville, Tennessee. He developed a particular fondness for Bluegrass and country music, which dominated the airwaves at the time, and he continues to enjoy Bluegrass to this day.

When Douglas was admitted to first grade in Pasadena, Texas, there was no special education available, making the experience frightening for him. Some of the other children made fun of him, and being away from home and family, he struggled to cope with the teasing and the unfamiliar environment.

By the time Douglas entered second grade, the school system was beginning to develop special education classes. He fondly remembers Miss Peterson, his teacher from second to sixth grade, who taught math, geography, history, and other standard subjects to her special education students, although there was no provision for Braille. The special education group was allowed to go out for recess, but they played only with each other in a corner of the schoolyard. The group wasn't exclusively for blind students, and they struggled with activities like jump rope due to coordination and vision challenges. Douglas really liked Miss Peterson, who was patient and had a great rapport with students with special needs.

At the age of seven, in 1951, Douglas was taken to Houston to see Dr. Richard E. Lee, an eye specialist. While cataract surgery had been performed for some time with varying results, the decision was made to operate on Douglas's left eye in hopes of improvement. After the surgery, he had to lie flat on his back for a whole week with a large dressing over his eye. He also had sandbags beside his head. Although the dressing itched, he was only allowed to scratch with the end of his elbow—a not very helpful solution. The surgery did lead to some limited improvement in his vision in that eye. At that time, it wasn't fully understood how much of his vision loss was due to changes in the brain from a lack of visual stimulation versus the impact of the cataract itself.

In 1952, Dr. Lee performed surgery on Douglas' right eye, and once again, he had to endure the discomfort of an eye patch and a week of bed rest. Although there was some improvement in his vision, it was not as substantial as the improvement in his left eye. By 1953, the gains in his vision had begun to diminish, leading to additional surgeries in both 1953 and 1954. Douglas vividly remembers the experience of undergoing these surgeries, particularly the use of ether as an anesthetic, which left him, like many others, feeling terribly nauseated afterward. Despite enduring four surgeries and all the associated trials and suffering, Douglas' vision remained significantly impaired. He could perceive light and some shapes but was unable to read or write.

Douglas grew up in an over-protective family that expected little from him. He had no chores, didn't clean his room, and rarely helped in the kitchen. He gained some independence by learning to ride a bike, but his parents accompanied him everywhere, even in public. He loved visiting electronics stores to ask questions, but his parents' constant presence limited his interactions and left him feeling unsure of himself, especially as he entered adulthood.

In 1958, at age thirteen, Douglas was enrolled in the Texas School for the Blind in Austin, Texas after finishing the sixth grade. Despite being thirteen and still in sixth grade due to five years in special education without braille instruction, his father's reluctance to admit his disability suggests significant family discussion before the decision. Nevertheless, his father drove the 160 miles to Austin and admitted him to the school.

Douglas and his father were first introduced to the school's superintendent before being assigned a dorm room. His father helped him move in and said his goodbyes, leaving Douglas on his own in Austin. His older roommates were supposed to teach him dorm life, but their help was limited. When Douglas failed to meet the neatness standards for his clothes, the dorm supervisor dumped his drawer on the floor, a common practice by the staff. He eventually learned to keep his clothes in order. Additionally, as punishment, he was required to "walk the pole" for two hours, holding a rod across his shoulders and walking for one hour per dumped drawer. This harsh, unexplained punishment was a sign of the challenges ahead.

Doug remembers the separation from his family as terrible, and he cried for over two weeks. Given the staff's harsh approach to interpersonal contact, it's no surprise the transition was rough. He wouldn't see his family again until Thanksgiving.

But kids adjust and the other students became Doug's family and friends, although they were also making their own adjustments. The staff, likely minimally trained and limited in number, provided little emotional support. Their primary role seemed to be enforcing rules and ensuring students toed the line. The students supported each other as best they could, but it was a traumatic experience for most during their first year.

In the first year, in 7th grade, Doug was introduced to the manual typewriter by his teacher, Mrs. Nance. She presented the keyboard and taught the class the location of the keys through verbal repetition. To help them learn, she used music in four-four time, having the students type three-letter words followed by hitting the space bar repeatedly in a rhythmic pattern: "one two three, space bar, one two three, space bar." Mrs. Nance was flexible about the words used, focusing instead on maintaining a steady tempo. This method helped the students develop a consistent rhythm and become proficient typists. Doug particularly enjoyed using the typewriter as it allowed him direct interaction with the sighted world. He has continued to use the typewriter in his adult life, notably for writing checks.

Overall, the students enjoyed the "village" environment where they learned and socialized, forming a close-knit group. However, this setting did not provide them with experience with the outside world. They were not taken on walks with a white cane to learn about navigating the streets of Austin or dealing with traffic. In the 1950s and 60s, the school was located near the northern edge of town. Perhaps there was insufficient staff to supervise such walks, or there was a lack of familiarity with the use of canes. Most significantly, there was no provision for interaction with the broader world, making the school an isolated "island" unto itself.

Originally, canes used by the visually impaired were black. In 1930, George Bonham, associated with a local Lion's Club in Illinois, suggested making the canes white with a red bottom to increase their visibility on streets and sidewalks. In 1944, a man named Hoover developed the standard practice of moving the cane from side to side to detect objects before walking into them. Despite these advancements, the majority of visually impaired people do not use a cane.

Perhaps the school did not teach cane usage for practical reasons. However, by the 1970s and 80s, it became common to see students walking along sidewalks, practicing using the cane, crossing streets at intersections, and being supervised by their instructor to learn about navigating the outside world.

The numerous strict rules on the campus were a significant drawback for the students. They were not allowed to leave the campus to explore other parts of Austin, and they couldn't even approach the sidewalk between the girls' and boys' dorms to interact more with female students. Holding hands was prohibited, and they were discouraged from walking with the opposite sex in the school halls, although this rule was hard to enforce. There were also many regulations about mealtime, including where one could sit, who would serve the food, when to get to the classrooms, when to be in the dorm room, and when the lights had to be turned out.

Despite the rules, students endlessly passed notes in class. If caught, the notes, including love notes, were read aloud to the class, but this did not deter them much. As is common with high school students, they often had crushes on their classmates, and it was very traumatic for them when these crushes ended.

The demanding school curriculum helped distract the students from homesickness. Large print books were available, and Doug began learning Braille. They used a slate and stylus to create the raised dots, pushing on the back of the slate and writing from right to left so the text was correctly oriented when turned over and read from the front. Doug quickly picked up Braille and, by the end of his first year, was learning some shorthand. Single letters were used as abbreviations for certain words, such as "W" for "will," "K" for "knowledge," and "L" for "like," which sped up the writing process.

There was a lot of reading in the classroom, and the school had a library full of books. Doug feels that, with more interest and effort, he could have nearly achieved a college-level education during high school.

One day, Doug heard someone playing the flute and was captivated by the sound. He managed to rent a flute from Strait Music and found a teacher, Shirley Fraiser, a member of the Austin Jazz Ensemble, to give him lessons. Doug took flute lessons for three years, but eventually, his teacher became unavailable, and he never returned to the instrument.

Doug also developed an interest in playing the piano. Lucille Gilmanot, the choir director, took him under her wing and gave him lessons. She would sit beside him, place his fingers on the keys, and explain which note he was playing. Doug's peripheral vision for shapes and shades helped him find middle C and orient himself on the keyboard. He learned a few simple tunes, but he has not had the opportunity to continue practicing the piano.

Although the initial separation from family was traumatic, the students eventually adjusted to the school. They enjoyed the camaraderie of their peers, who understood the shared handicap, and they developed lasting friendships. The school felt like a small "village" where they were the majority, free from being seen as "different" or facing bullying. In this enclave, they escaped societal judgment and found a supportive community.

During the school year, every other weekend, the students would gather on the outside basketball court or, in the winter, inside the gyms to socialize. Some students brought records, and they learned to dance to the music. Having never "seen" anyone dance, they were clumsy at first, but necessity fostered creativity, and they eventually learned.

Doug, due to his rather overprotected upbringing, lacked confidence in life. He didn't know how to dance and didn't realize that other students were equally inexperienced. As a result, he didn't enjoy the dances. One of the common punishments at the school was the removal of privileges, such as being banned from attending dances. On one occasion, Doug was forbidden to go to the dance for some infraction he doesn't remember. He didn't tell the staff that he was delighted by this punishment and ended up having the happiest evening in his own dorm room.

Though they enjoyed summers at home, they eagerly anticipated returning to school in the fall to reunite with friends. Doug, who had no friends in Pasadena, cherished his school friendships, especially with Rene Perez. He would wait on the dorm steps for Rene's return, and they'd celebrate by walking the campus or sharing summer stories in their rooms as they settled back into the school routine

On campus, they were required to sweep their dorm floors daily and mop on weekends, moving furniture to clean the corners. Occasionally, Doug, who had limited vision, would stand the mop upright in the middle of the room and leave. Soon, he'd hear it crash to the floor as Rene, who was totally blind, walked into it. It was these small pranks that brought them fun and more closeness.

Doug also formed a friendship with Allen Holcomb, with whom he often wandered around. Defying the rules, they cross 45th Street, which was the south edge of the campus, and walk five blocks south on Marathon Boulevard to Ballard's Icehouse, more for the adventure than for the gum they would buy. One evening, however, their excursion didn't go as planned. Mistaking the gutter for a sidewalk in the dim light, Allen stepped into water, soaking his shoes and pants.

Their adventures continued as they climbed the fence on the north side of the school to explore the nearby neighborhood. Though the area wasn't particularly exciting, they enjoyed the thrill of exploration. One night, while climbing back over the fence, Doug got his pants leg caught at the top and hung upside down, panicking at the thought of being caught. Whispering for help, he called Allen, who carefully unhooked him and helped him to the ground. Despite the complexity of their predicament, they surprisingly never got caught on any of their adventures.

Doug and Allen's adventurous spirit led them on another daring exploration. They discovered a small door at the end of Cottage E, which led to tunnels housing steam pipes for the heating system. Crawling on hands and knees, they explored the tunnels connecting various buildings, eventually reaching the main building across campus. Inside, they found access to a large auditorium with an organ and climbed to a platform above the pipes. Though they feared getting caught, no one discovered them. They even playfully acted out a scene on the stage. On one trip, Allen got his leg stuck between some pipes, but Doug helped him free without injury, and their secret remained safe.

The coffee in the cafeteria was terrible, but Doug drank it to fit in. Wanting better coffee, he asked Fred Tinnin, a house fellow, if he could use a hot plate in his apartment bathroom. As a house supervisor he had a separate apartment to himself. Surprisingly, Fred agreed. Doug set up a hot plate using a pull-chain current tap and extension cord in the bathroom light socket, and soon he was brewing his own coffee. It became a pleasure for him and his friends, and occasionally, he even brought his better brew to share with other students in the dining room.

The school shop offered vocational activities, including chair caning and making mops and brooms. Students learned to cane chairs, feeling the holes and weaving patterns with even tension. As they gained proficiency, they even provided the service to the public. Broom-making involved shredding corn stalks into thin strips using a machine with spiked drums. Though Doug struggled with the broom-making, he had another idea. One afternoon, he and Allen left a shop window open and later returned to collect shredded corn strands, attempting to smoke them. The taste was so awful they quickly abandoned the idea and never tried it again.

Allen was often the instigator of their adventures. One day, he and another student disappeared from school; Allen, from San Antonio, caught a bus home without permission. Typically, parents had to send a letter and a ticket for such trips, but none was received. When Allen returned to campus, unlike the other student who never came back, he was punished. He had to walk the pole for fifty hours, rain or shine, during any free time—a harsh penalty that likely didn't boost his fondness for the school.

To an outsider, the faculty's approach to student exploration at the school might seem unexpected. With ample free time, it's no surprise that students like Doug and Allen devised various ways to explore their surroundings. It's likely that many groups were exploring the campus during their downtime. Despite their adventures, Doug and Allen were never "caught." Given that they couldn't see who might be watching, it's possible the staff observed them but chose not to intervene. Perhaps the faculty recognized that these explorations were a necessary part of the students' development, allowing them to safely explore their world before venturing out beyond the school. It would seem only logical that students would explore as part of their development and to allow them some freedom would be part of the process of teaching.

Among the friends Doug made at school was Ann McMullen. They met at dances and shared some classes, dating occasionally during Doug's senior year, despite him being five years older. Their dates were mostly school dances since off-campus outings weren't practical. Ann's mother even remarked that Doug was "real cute."

The school's cook, a no-nonsense Norwegian woman, taught a cooking class where she demonstrated using a pressure cooker. When Doug asked what would happen if he removed the flapper valve as the steam built up, she replied, "Once you've cleaned the food off the ceiling, I'll take you outside and give you a spanking." At 22 and a senior, Doug found the threat inappropriate but chose not to respond. He suspected the cook never would have followed through on it.

Doug's uncle, his father's brother, lived in Austin while Doug attended school, but they had very little contact. Despite his mother's requests, the uncle rarely visited, always citing other commitments. This likely reflected the strong stigma surrounding disabilities at the time. Doug's father struggled to accept his son's blindness, making it difficult to ask his brother to visit the 'School for the Blind.' The uncle may have been uncomfortable interacting with Doug and the other students, reflecting the broader societal discomfort with disabilities. Acceptance of such differences was far from common back then, and perhaps it still is.

After graduating high school at 22 in 1966, Doug moved back home and began working at the Light House for the Blind in Houston, a non-profit providing training and employment for blind individuals. He was introduced to broom-making, which differed from his school experience, and quickly mastered operating a machine that drilled holes and stapled brush horsehair into broom heads. His proficiency, thanks to his familiarity with handling electronic equipment and other tools, allowed him to work faster than others, leading to jealousy from his supervisor. Doug thought that the supervisor was just another worker who had been promoted from Doug's level and he was concerned about Doug catching up with him.

Because the organization was a shelter for blind workers, Doug and other workers were paid less than minimum wage. Seeking better opportunities, he enrolled in an electronics assembly course, which included both electronics and mechanical assembly. There, he learned to solder, make extension cords, work on crystal radios, and use radio tubes, mastering various steps in the manufacturing process. His prior experience at home helped him quickly excel in the course.

Western Electric created a program to hire blind or visually impaired employees, and Doug was the only one he knew who was eventually hired. His job involved testing phone ringer mechanisms, which required meeting production quotas. Due to his limited vision, Doug developed his own methods for testing, but he was slower than sighted workers. His supervisor often pressured him to keep up with the quota, a common issue when employees are promoted to supervisory roles and enforce rules too strictly. Despite ten years of consistent work, union membership didn't offer much support against criticism. In 1979, feeling the stress of speed production and growing unhappy, Doug resigned from the company, leaving behind good pay and health insurance.

In retrospect, Doug sees his decision to quit as hasty and unwise. He gave up good wages, a solid retirement plan, and health benefits. Looking back, he believes that with greater maturity and self-confidence, he would have stayed, reaping the long-term benefits that would have significantly improved his senior years.

Doug developed a close friendship with Jerry Clever that eventually became a gay relationship. Living on Social Security disability, Doug and Jerry discovered that Baltimore, Maryland, offered excellent public transportation, convenient shops, and a vibrant entertainment scene. It was a long way from Texas but, in 1981, they moved there for a trial month and ended up staying in the welcoming community. Jerry found work in a nursing home, and they enjoyed socializing in gay bars like the Drinkery. They also frequented several local restaurants, particularly enjoying the excellent Baltimore crab cakes.

Doug experienced a significant breakthrough when he was supposed to meet Jerry at the Drinkery after work. Typically lacking self-confidence in social situations, he hesitated to go alone. As he was about to leave, he closed his front door, leaned against it, and symbolically pointed in front of him, saying to his shy alter ego, "You scared self can just stay here, and I am going out." With that, he opened the door and left with newfound confidence. This moment marked a positive shift in his life, as he felt he had taken a major step forward.

Everything seemed to be going well until 1984 when Jerry visited the doctor, and a chest X-ray revealed a lump. As a long-time smoker, Jerry was at risk, and a biopsy confirmed that he had lung cancer. He began radiation therapy, which included implants in his lungs. For several months, Jerry responded well to treatment and remained relatively stable. However, his condition eventually worsened as the disease progressed. As his health declined, he was hospitalized. Despite the medical efforts, there came a time when treatment was no longer effective. There was little more that could be done. In an attempt to maintain his weight and strength, a feeding tube was eventually placed in his stomach.

Jerry was determined not to die in the hospital, so he decided to go home. Hospice care was arranged, and a hospital bed was set up in his home. Doug took on the responsibility of providing total care, including administering liquid nutrition through the feeding tube. Hospice advised Doug that when Jerry passed, he should call them instead of 911. When the time came, they first called the priest, who came right away. However, when they contacted Hospice, no one arrived, and they eventually had to call an ambulance. In an effort to console Doug, the priest encouraged him to cry, shed many tears, and then get some rest. Doug followed his advice, and it brought him some comfort.

Jerry's passing severed Doug's connections in Baltimore, leaving him feeling unanchored without his longtime companion. Many of the local businesses and restaurants had either relocated or changed ownership, and the transportation system had undergone changes, making the town less convenient and familiar to him.

Later that year, Doug returned to Pasadena, realizing there was nothing left for him in Baltimore except painful memories. His sister assisted with the expenses of his move and helped cover the deposit on an apartment, which he later repaid. Feeling unsettled, Doug briefly returned to Baltimore for a few months, but the attempt proved futile as the place no longer held the sense of familiarity it once did.

Now in his forties, Doug took a job at Burger King in Pasadena, Texas to keep himself occupied. Although he enjoyed working at the grill and was good at it, he found himself reporting to a 'sassy young supervisor' who was inconsistent and seemed to lack respect for his age and experience.

One day, when work was slow, the supervisor assigned small cleaning tasks to the employees. Doug was tasked with cleaning a small refrigerator below the counter. Feeling somewhat weary and knowing the supervisor would closely inspect his work, he took on the task as a challenge. Doug meticulously cleaned every inch of the appliance, including the gasket on the door. When the supervisor inspected it, she declared it 'very clean,' and Doug felt satisfied that he had met the challenge.

On another occasion, the supervisor left the store to attend to other matters, leaving the young employees unsupervised. They decided to have a food fight in the kitchen. Although they cleaned up afterward, this incident was the last straw for Doug, and he decided to resign.

Doug's early life had been rather sheltered growing up in a very protected home environment, attending a cloistered School for the Blind, and starting his career quietly at Western Electric. These experiences left him ill-prepared for conflict. He had left Western Electric out of frustration with the job and now found himself leaving Burger King when things became chaotic.

In 1991, Doug moved back in with his parents. His father, who had grown up in the small East Texas town of Doucette, on the Louisiana border, wanted to return there after retiring from Arco in 1980. However, Doucette was a very small town with no services for Doug. His mother, seemingly sensing what was to come, asked Doug if he would stay and live in their house for a while if his father passed away. Tragically, his father suffered a massive stroke and died later that year. Doug stayed for six months, but with no bus transportation or other facilities in Doucette, he arranged to move to Austin. During this time, his only activity was attending the Episcopal church each week with a friend.

Although Doug had little tolerance for unpredictability, he did not wallow in self-pity. He chose to move on, remain active, and engage with people and places where he could find a sense of self-sufficiency and comfort within his community.

Doug completed his move to Austin, attracted by the city's good transportation, familiarity with available facilities, and a few friends who still lived there. The Commission for the Blind employed a secretary who was a valuable resource, providing Doug with contact information for people he knew. Once again, his sister stepped in to help with the move, as Doug still had some belongings in storage in Pasadena. He settled on Houston Street in Austin, knowing that Hancock Center, with its Sears and Roebuck, grocery store, restaurants, and other convenient shops, was nearby.

In Austin, Doug reconnected with friends from the School for the Blind who had also relocated to the city. In 1993, a former classmate, Josephine Fina, hosted a small reunion at her home. Doug took the bus to attend, joining seven other alumni, including Anne McMullen and her husband, who were living in Fort Worth at the time. He hadn't seen Anne in fifteen years. The group spent the day reminiscing about their school experiences, catching up on their lives since graduation, and discussing the common challenges they had faced and how they had overcome them; much like any other reunion. The event was a success, filled with laughter and shared memories, and it was particularly heartening for Doug to see how his peers had coped with their limitations. In retrospect, this reunion became a significant moment in Doug's life.

Now comfortably settled in Austin, Doug was not working because he received monthly Social Security disability payments. Employment opportunities for blind individuals were limited, as many businesses were unfamiliar with the skills they possessed. However, Doug had an expanding circle of friends with whom he spent time. An intriguing opportunity arose when Doug, along with several other graduates of the School for the Blind, learned about a program where they could tutor summer school students at the school. They provided braille lessons to students needing extra help. Doug's student was Dustin Pace, a teenager eager to better learn braille. They developed a close relationship, and Doug found great satisfaction in helping the younger generation.

One day, after a lesson, as they walked outside, Dustin unexpectedly asked, 'How did y'all get into the steam tunnels? Where did y'all go when you got in there?' These questions brought back memories of the lore that surrounded the students at the school, and Doug was more than happy to share the stories, likely inspiring further student exploration.

Doug observed that a distinct culture exists around schools for the blind, with stories from various schools sharing common themes. He had communicated with former students from different generations and states and found a surprising similarity in their experiences. These stories were so similar that it was hard to tell they occurred at different institutions, many miles apart. Even Ronnie Milsap, the famous singer who attended the Tennessee State School for the Blind, recounted in his autobiography how one teacher became so angry that he struck Ronnie, knocking him out of his desk and completely blinding the one eye in which he had retained a little vision. The teacher faced no consequences. Such tales of adventures and misadventures were a significant part of the students' experiences during their years at the school.

Ann McMullen

Ann Levae McMullen, born in 1949, is a descendant of the Hatfield family from the famous Hatfield-McCoy feud, that took place near the West Virginia and Kentucky border. Her mother, Mary

Britton, was raised in an orphanage in Corsicana, Texas, after losing her father to the 1918 flu epidemic. With a fourth-grade education, Mary's mother was unable to support her four children, leading to the family's placement in the state orphanage in Corsicana, where Mary grew up. Ann's father, Floyd McMullen, came from Mississippi and was one of ten children. As a child, he helped his father make bathtub gin, and after his mother died when he was a teenager, he and his siblings were conscripted into the family business of moonshine production. This environment led to chronic alcohol addiction for most of them. Despite these challenging beginnings, the McMullens, who had only high school educations, became avid readers and instilled a love of books in their three daughters. Floyd even taught himself higher math for fun.

"Floyd, I don't think she can see. Watch her eyes." Ann's mom waved her hand in front of her face as reported in the family lore. "Her eyes are moving, but not following your hand," responded her Dad, worry evident in his tentative tone. He clapped his hands once, and she jerked her head toward the sound. "She can hear, "he said, relieved. An appointment was made with the doctor who delivered her, and the blindness was confirmed. The cause unknown through many years.

On the way home they discussed the situation. One can only imagine the fear of this unknown that gripped them knowing they had no experience. But they had good common sense and had done well with their two older girls so, they just decided to use the same child rearing techniques as in the past. That turned out to be a great gift to Ann as it allowed for a certain freedom to explore her world with her two older sisters. She was three months old at this stage.

She seemed to be fearful when place in her crib, so she was allowed to sleep with Louise or Linda from a very young age, and that helped. When she started walking at age twelve months, Louise was allowed to take her for walks on the sidewalk and eventually they played on the swing that their father had made. When walking with her sisters the family watched from afar and all of their neighbor watched out for her as well. She says that she was confident of her play area and did not feel afraid of most things.

She learned to ride a bicycle in areas with no traffic and even mastered roller skating on the sidewalk by the age of three. Since

Ann had never 'seen' anyone skate, her father brought home a pair of skates and had her feel their shape, the wheels, and the clamps that held them on her shoes. He then guided her, first by holding her under her arms from behind, then by holding her hands in front, before eventually letting her skate on her own. Ann spent many days learning the boundaries of her skating range and identifying any obstacles that might be dangerous. She was never excluded from playing with her sisters and friends outside.

Ann recalls that her only fear was a storm drain in the curb down the street. One evening, at dusk, she bravely went to the drain, sat on its lid, and hung her legs down into the opening. Although terrified and shaking, she lasted about ten seconds before running for her life. Determined to conquer her fear, Ann returned to the drain every day for five days, gradually sitting for longer periods until she realized she was no longer frightened. Her mother, who had observed Ann's actions without interfering, noticed her daughter staying longer each day and understood that Ann was trying to overcome her fear. With Ann's determination and her mother's careful, non-intrusive support, Ann learned to face challenges in a safe and supportive environment.

Though adventuresome in many ways, eating was a problem. She seemed to have had an aversion to some foods. She found mealtime to be an unpleasant event until she was around age ten. She had a definite texture aversion. She found that the textures of certain foods were abhorrent and refused to eat anything that felt slimy to her. Apparently, this is somewhat common with young blind children. She would develop a mild nausea at the thought of many meals and could not explain it verbally so, was just reluctant to eat anything. She became averse to meat, chicken, and fish, pasta, dumplings, cheese, cooked greens (slimy) of any kind.

And then she hated it if any of her foods touched any other food on her plate. So, her mother built little walls between the food with crusts of bread. She thinks that since she could not see what food was on her plate, she would sometimes mix one food with another and create a disgusting mess. She did, however, outgrow these problems as an early teen and took another major step when going to the School for the Blind and eating in the cafeteria.

Ann's dad always wanted her to experience the world as he did. When they drove through the countryside, he would often stop the car, take her out of the back seat, and lead her into a field. There, he would guide her hands to feel the crop from its stem all the way to the top, explaining what it was, how it grew, how it was harvested, and what it was used for before returning to the car. He also took her to museums, where he obtained permission for her to touch certain items, explaining their significance and why they were displayed.

Thanks to this early instruction, she was an eager student when she began kindergarten at age five in Fort Worth, Texas. Her young teacher, who had never taught a blind student before, was imaginative and compassionate, helping Ann to thrive. Ann was placed in a class with sighted students, where her teacher guided her to her desk and allowed her to explore it with her hands. The teacher introduced Ann to her classmates, and she began learning to recognize their voices and associate them with their names.

In Fort Worth, blind students from first through sixth grade attended one elementary school, where two "brilliant" women made school enjoyable for Ann. She spent half of her day in the special education section, learning adaptive skills like Braille and using different tools for math. The other half of the day was spent with sighted students, where she continued to learn standard subjects and further developed the math and writing skills introduced in special education. As close older sisters often do, Linda taught Ann how to write in print while she was in third grade. By fourth grade, Ann learned to type.

A major crisis struck during her fifth-grade year when her father was diagnosed with chronic obstructive pulmonary disease, a progressive loss of lung function caused by smoking. His illness was severe enough that he was advised to quit his job as a special delivery messenger for the U.S. Postal Service in Fort Worth. Despite being eligible for Social Security disability insurance, the family faced a six-month waiting period before payments would begin, leaving them "destitute," as Ann described it. Friends provided housing and food to help them through this difficult time. The following year, they moved to a small dairy farm outside of town, made known to them by friends. Although the prognosis indicated that her father had only about a year to live, her parents chose not to share this information with the girls.

In the summer of 1959, when Ann turned eleven, plans were made for her to enroll in the Texas School for the Blind in Austin, Texas. As part of the admission process, the family received a letter listing the items she needed to bring to school. The Junior League of Austin also donated many items to the school, which were made available to students as needed. Her parents must have had heavy hearts as they drove her to Austin. After enrolling her, helping her unpack in the girls' dorm, and giving her advice about living with a roommate—like not touching other students' belongings—they drove home. According to her mother, her father grieved for two weeks.

After her parents left, the reality of where she was and how lonesome she felt suddenly hit her, and she cried. She was assigned to a room with two other students. Being the first to arrive, she was allowed to choose her bed, closet, and dresser. Soon, a girl came to make friends and showed her around the campus. That was all it took; she never really felt homesick again as she made new friends. It seemed that the wonderful early training by her parents and her good teachers had made the transition to a new learning environment relatively easy. That first night, lying on her side in her new bed, she realized that if she sucked her thumb, as she usually did, someone would hear. That was the end of that comforting habit, and she soon didn't miss it.

Unlike Doug, Ann was instructed by other students on how to neatly organize her clothes in the drawers, which had already been a habit at home. Her creative mother always made her clothes because money was tight. Thoughtfully, her mother used distinctly different materials for each dress so Ann could identify the color by touch. Later, around age thirteen, her mother made her blouses and skirts, always adding something unique, like a special button, clip, or pleats, so Ann could easily match her outfits. Dressing in coordinated colors and patterns was never a problem. And she always wore penny loafers that didn't require tying.

In her early days at the school, Ann quickly learned the daily routine. They woke up at 6:30 a.m., dressed, and were ready for breakfast by 7:00 a.m. After breakfast, they returned to their rooms to sweep the floor and dust the furniture and radiator. This routine was taught to her by another student, but a house parent would come by to check that everything was done. There was no praise for a job well done, only punishment if things weren't satisfactory or if something inappropriate was said.

On her first day of class, her teacher, Mr. Gorham, didn't call her name during roll call. Since she wasn't on the list, she was sent to the principal's office, which she was told was at the end of the hall. Unsure of which direction to go, she chose to turn right. At the end of the hall, she found a room and felt a glass door. Since no one was there, she waited. After what seemed like a long time, Mr. Cusher finally arrived and confirmed that she had been assigned to that class. She returned to the classroom feeling a bit more confident—she had successfully navigated the hall, found the office, and completed her task. It was one more triumph in her daily learning.

Ann found a certain satisfaction in her meals. Although she had always been a picky eater, the limited choices at the school forced her to adapt. She told herself she would have to eat whatever the other students ate to avoid standing out. To her surprise, she soon realized she liked many of the foods she had previously avoided. Her finicky eating habits quickly disappeared.

In the first days at school, students were assigned a table and seat in the dining hall, and these assignments remained the same throughout the school year. Each table seated eight students— three on each side and one at each end. The two students sitting in the middle seats on the sides were chosen because they had some eyesight. They were tasked with retrieving the dishes of food, which were then placed family-style on the table. These students would describe the dishes to the others, who would then use their fork, knife, or sometimes their fingers to confirm what was what.

Ann felt that having the same students perform these tasks every day was a form of discrimination against both the partially sighted and the totally blind students. However, she recognized that it made life easier for the staff, that was likely the main reason for this arrangement.

Each day, one table was designated for clean-up and dishwashing duties. With eight students per table, the tasks were divided: two students soaked the dishes in a special solution, two washed, two dried, and two set the tables for the next meal. These chores were essential not only for the school's budget but also as valuable learning tasks for the students.

Eating is one of the most challenging tasks for blind individuals. While you can touch a pencil, a handrail, or a piece of clothing and easily identify it, touching food can be messy, distasteful, or even painful if it's hot. Cutting chicken off the bone with a knife is nearly impossible without seeing the shapes and textures. Eating small, round items like cherry tomatoes is another challenge—stabbing them with a fork is impractical since they tend to roll away unseen. Ann prefers to pick them up with her fingers at home and avoids ordering them in restaurants. Green beans are similarly difficult to manage with a fork, so there are certain foods she won't order when dining out. It's also hard to tell if something falls off your plate, which can lead to a messy meal. According to Ann, the boys are generally less neat in their eating habits.

Blind children quickly develop their other senses. Ann, for instance, could listen to the sounds of a room or hallway and easily orient herself. She had little trouble navigating stairs and, as an exuberant child, often walked up and down without using the handrail. When excited, she would even jump two steps at a time, both ascending and descending.

During that first year, disaster struck. Her aunt and uncle visited the school to deliver heartbreaking news: her father had passed away from his lung disease on December 6th. Ann sat on her uncle's lap as he held her tightly, and they made arrangements to take her home early for Christmas and the funeral. The meal in the cafeteria before she left was unusually quiet. The house mother had informed the other students of her father's death and asked them to remain silent during the meal.

Ann stayed home for several weeks over Christmas. Before returning to school, her wise mother mentioned that it seemed she hadn't fully grieved her father's loss during her time at home. She warned Ann to expect some difficulties, perhaps even an illness, once she was back at school. Sure enough, about a week after her return, Ann developed a fever of 102. She was placed in the student infirmary, where she rested under the care of Dr. Happy Scott, an older general practitioner from town. She was kept in bed for three days after her fever subsided and spent much of that time crying. In retrospect, she realized this was exactly what her mother had anticipated.

Ann's early years at home, where she was allowed a great deal of independence, had helped her develop resilience. She grew to love being at the school, made many friends, and began to feel at home. She enjoyed the various activities and appreciated the strong educational support available to blind students. Ann especially liked her Spanish, Science, and Language Arts classes. She excelled as a student and was inducted into the National Honor Society in her senior year.

Ann had grown up with a love of music, and while in high school, she joined the choir. Since few students could read music, the songs were taught by memorization. In 1965, the school integrated, and the music teacher, Lucille Gilmanot, an African American woman, brought a lot of fun and energy to the choir. Ann sang with the choir throughout her four years of high school.

Despite the joy Ann found in learning and music, her social interactions with the staff or any form of adult guidance were almost non-existent. To her, it seemed that no adults at the school cared personally for the students. The staff was mainly concerned with enforcing the many rigid and often excessive rules. There were no personal relationships, no adults to turn to for help with homework or personal issues. For the girls, there was no one to guide them through the onset of their first period or to assist them in obtaining feminine hygiene products. The students had to rely on each other for support. Fortunately, Ann's family had prepared her well, making her transition relatively smooth.

One incident stood out to Ann. After a student experienced a traumatic event at home during a vacation, she struggled upon returning to school and was often in tears. A gym teacher consoled her with a hug—a rare act of kindness in a setting where such personal gestures were uncommon. Ann worried that the staff might disapprove of this act, as it was a time long before the era of sexual harassment policies. Given the general lack of closeness between the staff and students, it was hard to predict how the staff would react to such a gesture.

Students were taught various practical skills, with some taking cooking classes where they also learned table manners. These lessons, available to only a few students, including Doug and a few female students, covered proper use of silverware, table settings, serving etiquette, and the importance of waiting for everyone before starting a meal. It's surprising these valuable lessons weren't offered to all students.

An adventurous incident occurred when six students, including Ann, returned to school by bus from the Dallas/Ft. Worth area after the holidays. They decided to go to a movie, leaving their suitcases in the bus station lobby. Upon returning, they were reprimanded by Mr. Hall, an administrator, for leaving their belongings unattended, and letters were sent to their parents. Ann's practical mother likely questioned the fuss.

When asked if the girls ever explored the pipes under the building, Ann responded, "Goodness, no." The girls were too afraid of getting caught. However, there was a scandal when some girls secretly invited their boyfriends into their dorm at night. When discovered by the house mother, the students involved were expelled, shocking many of the other girls.

During Ann's senior year, the school hired an instructor specialized in Orientation and Mobility training. He introduced the use of canes for blind students, taking them on walks around campus and nearby streets to teach safe navigation, including crossing streets at traffic lights. Ann has used a cane ever since.

After graduating from high school in 1967, Ann had hoped to attend college, but she struggled with Algebra I and realized that pursuing higher education wasn't feasible. Knowing she needed to find a job and eventually move out of her parents' home, she became a client of the Texas Commission for the Blind, where she explored various educational and job training options.

Ann chose to participate in a federally sponsored program that trained students to manage eateries in public office buildings. The training was provided at the Light House for the Blind in Houston, leading to her first job managing a small snack shop in a car dealership. However, due to her age—she wasn't yet 21— she wasn't allowed to run the shop independently because it sold cigarettes. This setback led her back to training, this time as a medical transcriptionist, a field she worked in for a couple of years.

At age 20, Ann finally secured the job she had wanted: running the coffee shop on her own. She enjoyed the work, especially interacting with customers, and took pride in making hamburgers, sandwiches, and selling snacks and cigarettes.

Around this time, she became pregnant by her high school boyfriend, Tony. Unwilling to tell her mother that she was pregnant and unmarried, they quickly had a justice of the peace marriage before breaking the news. Their first child, Alan, was born in August 1969. When Alan was two, Ann and Tony moved back to Fort Worth to be closer to her family, which provided support with childcare so she could continue working. However, the marriage ended as they realized they were not compatible.

In Fort Worth, Ann was selected to manage a large cafeteria in a federal center, a position she held for five years. During that time, she remarried and, in 1976, gave birth to her daughter, Kindra. Ann became a full-time homemaker, dedicating herself to raising her children and caring for the home.

In 1982, when Alan was 15 and Kindra was six, Ann began volunteering at the county hospital. She ran errands, took lab results over the phone, and assisted with various tasks needed by the staff. Volunteering brought her joy, especially through her interactions with people and the sense of contributing to her community. Ann felt strongly that the public often underestimated the skills of people who are blind, noting that only about 30% of blind individuals are employed due to misconceptions about their abilities.

After three years as a volunteer, Ann took a job as a receptionist at the Fort Worth Lighthouse for the Blind, where she worked for five years. These were challenging times in her personal life. Her son, Allen, became involved with drugs and was incarcerated for possession, while her daughter, Kindra, also struggled with drugs and alcohol, hindering her progress. Ann's husband spent most of his time watching television, further contributing to the household tension. This turmoil led to their divorce in 1993, as Ann felt a strong need for a significant change.

Fortunately, not all the chaos persisted. Allen eventually turned his life around after prison, channeling his artistic talents into a successful career as a car body painter, though he sadly passed away at 53 from a heart attack. Kindra also straightened out her life, became a Christian, married, and moved to California, where her husband continued his career as a corporate pilot. Although she still occasionally struggled with alcohol, Kindra found stability through various jobs, including running her own dance studio. Eventually, she and her second husband relocated to Montana, where they found a more peaceful life.

Seeking a fresh start, Ann moved back to Austin, away from the turmoil in Fort Worth. Austin offered a supportive blind community, many of whom were friends from her school days. The city's resources and employment opportunities for the blind made it an ideal place for her to rebuild her life. Ann registered with the Texas Commission for the Blind and participated in a career exploration program at the Chris Cole Rehabilitation Center. Following the program, she was hired as a clerical assistant, becoming a typist for the psychologists and psychiatrist at the center, where she was the first blind person to hold that position. This role aligned with her previous experience as a medical transcriptionist.

In Austin, Ann reconnected with Doug Foxworth, a former high school sweetheart she hadn't seen in 25 years. Doug helped her navigate the city, teaching her bus routes and showing her the locations of essential places like stores and banks. With his assistance, she rented an apartment in the same complex where Doug lived, and he introduced her to the Episcopal Church, where she joined the choir and became an active member. Their rekindled romance led to marriage on April 22, 1995, with the church choir organizing their reception.

After five years as a typist, Ann was promoted to a teaching position. She developed a finishing program for students who had completed the career exploration course at the Texas Commission for the Blind. This program taught students how to apply the skills they had learned by completing a project. After successfully establishing that program, Ann transitioned to the braille translation unit, where she worked as a braille transcriber for two years.

As a transcriber, Ann utilized a software program called the "Duxbury Braille Translator" to produce Braille documents, that were then printed as hard copies for staff use. These documents became an integral part of the curriculum for blind individuals enrolled with the Texas Commission for the Blind. Ann truly loved this job because it allowed her to create new materials and facilitate innovative methods that positively impacted people's futures. She took great pride in ensuring that Braille education was accessible across a broad area of the state, knowing that her work played a vital role in shaping the lives of others.

In her continued exploration of the working world, Ann took on another role with the Texas Commission for the Blind, this time as the statewide Braille consultant. The program was brand new, and she was given complete responsibility for developing and managing it. Her mission was to promote the teaching of Braille to clients across the state and to ensure that teachers in all the field offices were competent in Braille instruction. Ann found this role to be exciting, challenging, and rewarding. It involved extensive travel, hard work, and the creation of a Braille curriculum that continues to be used fifteen years later. She considers this some of her best work, as the curriculum addresses many of the unique challenges that adults face when learning Braille.

Throughout her job as a statewide braille consultant, Ann was accompanied by three "seeing eye dogs". These loyal and loving companions were invaluable in her travels across the state and to various Commission offices. She still fondly remembers them as wonderful friends who provided both practical assistance and emotional support.

Ann retired in 2011 but soon embarked on a new adventure. After visiting several churches over the years, including the Episcopal church where she and Doug were married in 1995, and a Methodist church, they found a welcoming community at St. John's Episcopal Church. The warmth of this community inspired Ann to propose starting a Braille ministry. This ministry involved creating a weekly Braille bulletin for the service, which included the order of worship, hymns, and responsive readings.

To make this possible, Ann requested a digital copy of the bulletin from the church each week. Using the "Duxbury Braille Translator" software on her home computer and a 55-pound Braille printer in her bedroom, she prints out 20-page documents that allow blind congregants to actively participate in the service. This transition from passive listening to active involvement has been a significant contribution to the spiritual lives of the blind members of the congregation. This printed material even included the hymns for the service.

Ann has been providing this service for almost ten years, driven by her strong advocacy for blind services. The Braille ministry has drawn more blind congregants to the church, where they have found both faith and a supportive community. Ann's dedication has not only enriched her life but has also empowered others to fully engage in their worship.

Ann's marriage to Doug has been a comfortable and fulfilling partnership. She is the dynamo, full of energy and drive, while Doug is the quieter one, providing balance to their relationship. Over the years, they purchased two homes they were very fond of, always ensuring they were close to public transportation for easy access. Now, as renters, they appreciate the reduced responsibility of home upkeep, which has made life more manageable.

Their connection to the church community remains strong. A fellow church member who drives past their area regularly picks them up on the way to services. This arrangement not only ensures they attend church comfortably but also gives them a chance to visit and stay connected with their church family.

Although Doug is the more reserved of the two, he has kept himself actively engaged in the community. In the 1990s, a radio station specifically for blind listeners was established by Charles Rankin with a grant from the National Telecommunications and Information Agency to the Austin Council for the Blind. This station became a vital resource, providing news, reading newspapers, journals, and other material, along with public information and announcements tailored to a blind audience.

Mr. Rankin, who was deeply protective and even possessive of the station, closely guarded its operations. Sadly, when Mr. Rankin passed away in 1997, there was no one prepared to take over the station's management, leading to its closure and the station going off the air.

Doug, well-known to the Austin Council for the Blind and with a long-standing interest in radio, was appointed to manage the station following Mr. Rankin's passing. He took on several critical tasks to revitalize the station:

- **Negotiating Space**: Doug secured a new location for the station within the Texas School for the Blind, moving it from its previous rented space on Airport Boulevard, and integrating it into the School for the Blind.
- **Broadcasting Agreements**: He worked with the University of Texas radio station, KUT, to secure airtime and acquire a broadcast frequency. This involved establishing a connection cable to KUT and ensuring ongoing air space for the station.
- **Recruiting Volunteers**: Doug also focused on recruiting volunteers to read the content on air. Many of these volunteers were recruited through public service advertisements on KUT.

Doug's efforts helped ensure the station's continued operation, providing a valuable resource to the blind community.

The National Telecommunications and Information Agency (NTIA) once again provided the financial support needed to restart the radio station, contributing $40,000, with an additional $10,000 from the local council. When the station was re-launched, it was given the name "Austin Information Radio" (AIR), allowing them to brand themselves with the catchy phrase, "This is AIR on the AIR."

The funding also included money for purchasing specialized radios. These radios were uniquely designed to be tuned to a single frequency, a sub-frequency of the public station KUT, and did not allow listeners to change stations. These radios were distributed to the audience through the Austin Council for the Blind.

Doug played a central role in the daily operations. He would arrive at the station before noon and kick off the programming with the announcement: "You are now listening to Austin Information Radio. This is Douglas Foxworth asking you to stay tuned for Diane Dorman," or another volunteer reader, "who will be reading selected articles from today's edition of the Austin American Statesman." This marked the start of a day's programming that would continue until 8 P.M., with various volunteers reading throughout the day.

The volunteers, numbering around forty, were essential to the station's success. Doug personally recruited and trained them, conducting auditions to assess their reading skills and radio voice. Volunteers would select and read articles, ensuring they provided the full context by stating the source, date, and author before reading the entire piece. Even advertisements from grocery stores were read to ensure the blind audience could access the same information as sighted individuals. However, volunteers were strictly prohibited from editorializing or injecting personal opinions into the readings, maintaining the station's commitment to impartial information.

At 8 P.M., Doug would sign off with, "This is Douglas Foxworth signing off, and I will be switching you to a satellite feed from St. Paul, Minnesota for the program, Radio Talking Books, which will continue until noon tomorrow." The station would then resume its local broadcasting at noon each day of the week and not on the weekend. Doug's dedication ensured that AIR provided a valuable service to the blind community, keeping them informed and connected.

Ann and Doug's journey exemplifies resilience, creativity, and dedication in the face of challenges. Both have navigated the complexities of life as blind individuals, contributing significantly to their communities in distinct and impactful ways. Ann's passion for braille education led her to develop statewide programs and continue her advocacy through a Braille ministry at her church, enriching the spiritual lives of many. Doug, despite being more reserved, took on the immense task of reviving and managing Austin Information Radio, a vital resource for the blind community, demonstrating his ability to innovate and lead.

Their achievements highlight the unique skills and perspectives that Ann and Doug bring to the world. Ann's ability to take on challenges head-on, coupled with Doug's thoughtful and persistent approach to his work, has allowed them both to make lasting contributions. Whether through braille education, radio broadcasting, or simply living their lives with determination, they have set a powerful example of how to overcome barriers and make a difference.

At Drive a Senior Austin, Texas, we've had the privilege of supporting this dynamic couple, providing transportation and assisting them with technology as needed. One of our own volunteers who had special computer skills has assisted them in using their own computers as they have encountered difficulties. Their involvement in our activities, such as games day, and Octoberfest has added to the richness of our community. Ann and Doug's story is a reminder of the strength and creativity that individuals can bring to their communities, regardless of the challenges they face. We are honored to be part of their journey and look forward to continuing to support them in their active and inspiring lives.

Born into the War
Bergstrom, Elfie

In 1937, Austria saw the clouds of instability in the skies over Germany to the north. Hitler had been installed as chancellor in 1934 and his anti-Semitic and militaristic actions over the next three years were progressively more drastic. Schutzstaffel (SS) chief, Himmler, consolidates the state police into the Gestapo. And later formalizes the SS takeover of the concentration camp system. Increased anti-Semitism in Poland coincides with anti-Semitic laws passed at Nuremberg. 1936 the SS creates the Death Shield Division to guard concentration camps. In defiance of the Versailles Treaty, German troops occupy Rhineland. Arabs kill nine Jews in Jaffa. Two Palestinians and two others are killed by police during a general strike in Palestine in protest against Jewish immigration. Europe becomes even more unstable as German and Italian militaries become involved in the Spanish civil war between Francisco Franco and Republicans of the government.

1937 included the signing of a military pact between Germany and Japan and the Japanese army launches the massacre of Nanking as the first military act of World War II. And in 1938 Austria was annexed into Nazi Germany with the support of the general population.

Elfie Richter was born into this world in Graz, Austria in 1937, a country so poor following their involvement with Germany in the first world war that when reparation payments were levied against Germany, Austria was not required to make any payments. To add to the difficulties for her family, this was a birth out of wedlock. The father had been killed in the Airforce during the pregnancy, so no confirmation of a wedding was possible. There was no financial support from the military as the relationship was not formally recognized. At the time of Elfie's birth, the father had not been notified that his girlfriend was even pregnant. It is unclear to the family where the father was lost. It was a complicated mess from which Elfie's mother never completely seemed to extract herself.

The history of that time notes that Austria was not in any conflict but was under the stipulation of the Treaty of Versailles. Germany and Italy were involved in Spain's revolution. Germany did not invade Poland until 1939. There was no actual conflict in which it is reasonable to assume Elfie's father was involved in the air force in 1937. There are just no answers relative to how he died.

Elfie's father had been orphaned as a child and was raised by an uncle and aunt. They were strong Catholics and were set on having him become a priest. He chose not to follow that path and was therefore put out of that family's home because he was "not being cooperative." He signed up for the Airforce instead and may have remained the black sheep of the family.

According to the terms of the Treaty of Versailles, neither Germany nor Austria were allowed to develop certain military capabilities of infantry troops, naval forces, size and numbers of cannons, or maintaining submarines. In addition, Germany was to release control of a number of their foreign colonies. In defiance of the treaty, Germany began to develop more troops and built up their armed forces. This clandestine activity was going on in the early 1930's even before Hitler took over in 1934. Austria, as well, started defying the terms of the treaty and acquired airplanes from Italy and building up their military.

With the terrible economics of that time, Elfie's mother, Obilly "Tilly" Richter, found it difficult to find a job to support herself and her daughter. She asked her sister to care for Elfie and worked as a housekeeper for a couple of families in Vienne and Nurnberg, Austria from 1931 – 1938. She eventually chose to move to Holland in 1938 where she found work as a cook with a family and then took a job as cook and an assistant to a doctor. That lasted until 1942 after the invasion of the Netherlands by the Germans in 1940. With the entry of German control, Elfie's mother was conscripted into the German Army as a civilian worker assigned to a clerical position to a job keeping track of navy ships; listing those that left port, those that returned and those that did not, and the troop casualties. In 1944, the war was changing, and she was sent to Fehrenkrug, Germany to the artillery Arsenal as a civilian employee.

As the war finally ended, Tilly transitioned to working as a clerk and cook for the British until 1946. She returned to Austria in 1946 and lived with her sister and daughter for a time. Eventually she found a job as a housekeeper and cook for a Mr. Temple in Vienna. Life was quite complicated and unstable, so for a more stable living she took a job as housekeeper and assistant to Dr. Kanzler in Rehetobel, Switzerland. There was little contact or closeness to Elfie. The doctor was friends with a Mr. Bruggmann, who was the Swiss Minister to the United States. Eventually, Tilly applied for a position with Mr. Bruggmann and got the job. That led to a trip to the U.S. where she applied for and was granted a path to stay. It is documented in some records that she returned to Austria for a visit with her daughter and family in 1951 when Elfie was fourteen.

Meanwhile, Elfie was raised by her aunt (her mother's half-sister) and husband, Rose and Yacef Grubhotz, in Kalsfdorf, a small village three to four kilometers south of Graz. Graz was the second largest city in Austria behind Vienne.

In Kalsfdorf, her uncle Yacef was a blacksmith who worked for a company that made door handles and locks, and other hardware. The company provided living quarters for employees in eight nearby apartment buildings. The building had a broad, white, stucco front with a set of stairs indented into the front. There were balcony type porches all across the front onto which the doors of the apartments opened. It appears that there would have been a good chance for community interaction as each apartment opened onto this common porch and everyone would have walked on the porch to get to the common stairs.

Their apartment was on the third floor of the four-story building that was built in 1905. It had a kitchen area, one bedroom and a bathroom of sorts. The bathroom consisted of a separate closet like structure just outside the door of the apartment. The bedroom, not surprisingly for that time period, had no closets so clothes were placed in an armoire or chest of drawers. There was no running water in the building so water was hauled from the ground floor hand pump up to their apartment. The water was used in the kitchen and some bathing and laundry. There was a wooden tub in which they washed themselves and also washed clothes. They did not have a modern bathtub.

The stove was heated with wood or coal. Coal would have to be found around the factory where it was used for heating steel for the hardware they made in the foundry. Wood was more commonly used for fuel. They worked with a farmer to take down dead trees, split the wood and bring it home. On many occasions they would make an arrangement to have the farmer bring the wood to the apartment in his wagon.

Laundry was done in the apartment and some in the basement. It hung outside on a clothesline that consisted of a rope and pulley system between two buildings. Used water was then discarded in the toilet. That was then flushed down the drain into a collection cesspool in the basement. Periodically a farmer would come and empty the cesspool into a container on a trailer and transport it to the farm where it was used on his farm for fertilizer. The smell of fresh produce must have been refreshing.

The eight apartment buildings had small areas for a garden for the tenants. There Elfie remembers helping her aunt pull weeds and plant their vegetables and flowers. She remembers planting and gathering potatoes. They also grew cauliflower, cabbage, carrots, garlic and onions. The plot was quite small, so the number of vegetables was limited. The family helped on a farm nearby where they milked cows and did some weeding and crop picking. Farm labor was hard to find as more and more men were taken into the military. The public was allowed to pick up loose potatoes or glean from the farm after the major portion of the crop was plowed up for harvesting.

Yacef would take Elfie on walks in a buggy when she was small. One day they went for a walk around the village. Elfie went to sleep with the motion of the buggy. Apparently, Yacef was sleepy also and put the buggy beside him and laid down on the grass for a little nap. A couple of the women from the village came by and noted that Yacef was asleep. They decided to play a trick on him and took Elfie home with them. When he awoke and found her gone, he was in a complete panic. The story leaves out how he found Elfie, but he was rather upset when he found her at home.

One season the farmers were quite concerned about a potential blight of potato bugs. Some of the children from the school were taken to the fields to look at the potatoes and see if they could identify the bugs. Generally, potatoes are planted by cutting out the eyes of a potato and planting that segment in the ground. In that manor they can get a number of potato plants from one potato. The children would look at whole potatoes before they were cut to see if bugs were present. The exercise proved to be fairly effective.

When Elfie was five in 1942, Rose and Yacef, whom she referred to as mother and dad, had a baby boy, Werner. Elfie was moved down to a neighbor's apartment to stay for the several days of the delivery which was attended at home by a midwife. As she got a little older, she remembers having to wash some of his diapers. The children became very close and played around the apartment and in the yard. They often played soccer and Elfie generally played goalie. The children also made mud pies although they did not have a small stove in which they could be baked.

The generosity of the family lead them to take in another child, Egbert, the son of Rose's other sister. The economics of the time were quite difficult following World War II so there were many family disruptions. As they needed more room, a wall was taken down between their apartment and the next so that a second bedroom was provided for the children. There was a single lady living next door who did not need that room.

Christmas was a time she remembers as fun in this close-knit family. They started the holiday season with a celebration on December 6, St Nicholas day. St. Nicholas day was a remembrance of the young man in fourth century Turkey who gave away gifts to others. In Austria, the story went that he would come with gifts of figs for the good children. The fable included the part where he was accompanied by the devil who withheld figs from the little children who had been bad. On December 24th Christmas eve, they held the next event when the family sat down for dinner. The meal consisted of schnitzel, (veal dipped in egg, dusted with flour, dipped again in egg whites, covered with breadcrumbs and fried in deep lard or oil), potatoes or another vegetable. At the end of the meal, father would pull a string that went under the door to the bedroom where a bell would ring and the Christmas tree, with real candles, would be sitting. Under the tree would be the gifts from Santa. Even now Elfie wonders about the danger of the lighted candles on the tree unattended in another room. Since they had cut their own tree in the local forest it was at least fresh and less apt to catch fire.

A typical gift for children at Christmas was an apron worn daily by most Austrian children, particularly the girls. This was worn to protect the clothes children worn daily. Since everything was hand washed, keeping the clothes as clean as possible was very important. And the apron would be more easily washed. Aprons were worn by the girls through grade school but not to high school. Another common gift was a game that all the children could play, thus fewer individual gifts as money was limited.

In the apartment building there was a basement for washing clothes and a little storage area for each family. In addition, there was some storage space in the attic. Apparently, some time before one Christmas, Elfie had visited the attic and noted a small scooter. On Christmas eve when all the gifts had been opened, Elfie said, "what about the scooter in the attic?" Well, her parents had put it up there and forgotten about it. So, they went up and got it as the completion of her Christmas gifts. She got scolded for peaking in the attic just before Christmas.

The final celebration of the season was Epiphany, the celebration of the arrival of the three Wise Men as the first revelation of Christ to gentiles. This was celebrated by the family with parties or gatherings of neighbors where beef schnitzel was served and where there was music and dancing. Schnitzel, in the German/Austrian tradition, involved a veal cutlet, pounded until tender, breaded, and fried, similar to an American chicken fried steak. Other foods included canned vegetables. Many of the community had worked hard preparing and canning food from their own gardens. In addition, some produce was purchased from vendors or from farmers who would come to town with carts full of produce, sometime including apples, grapes, or peaches and pears in season.

71

Elfie, rather surprisingly, does not remember much about breakfasts on regular days. She thinks they had bread and milk. Lunch at school was a sandwich carried in the bag with her books. They did not have a separate lunch bag as that would have been too expensive. At Sunday dinner they had meat which was ordered at the butcher on Saturday afternoon and stored in the refrigerator of the butcher that evening. The butcher had the only refrigerator in town. On Sunday morning, before church, the meat would be picked up at the butcher and taken home to cook later. They would then go to church.

Elfie started school in Kalsdorf with about 20 kids in her class. The building was brick, as were most building in town. It was built in the early 1900's. There were two floors and each grade had a separate classroom. She liked most of her teachers and found school pleasant in general.

In the town was a hill on which was build a tall clock tower that co-existed as a watch tower in this completely walled village. When the children occasionally skipped school they frequently went to the hill and the tower to play and enjoy the open air and the view.

Elfie, at home and comfortable with her aunt and uncle, stayed in Kalsdorf in spite of the comings and goings of her mother. These were terribly chaotic times with families separated by war, shortages of everything, work hard to find and great uncertainty for most. Elfie was six in 1943. Europe was burning. Military trucks were coming and going on every street. The economy was almost unworkable, and jobs were nowhere and everywhere changed. Food was unreliably available and home gardens were the people's salvation. In addition to the vegetables they had chickens, rabbits and hedge hoggs. When the chickens quit laying then would go into the pot. The hedge hoggs were kept to help control rats and mice. When the hedge hoggs got old they also went into the pot. Apparently, the fat of the hedge hogg from under the skin was used as a suave for burns. Elfie fell on the stove one time and they put the fat on her chest burn. She has no scar, which she attributes to the fat as a sauve.

Elfie remembers waiting in bread lines and occasionally getting to the end of the line where no more bread was available. There was no sugar available so artificial sweetener, saccharin, was the only substitute. Elfie never learned to like that.

Her mother was moving about, looking for work, concerned about her daughter, stable in the knowledge of support by her sister and under the work orders of the German military in Holland and then Germany.

When the war was finally over, work continued to be difficult to find locally. She eventually went to Vienna for a job cooking for a family by the name of Temple. Surprisingly mobile, she moved to Switzerland to work for a Dr. Kanzler at home and also helped in his office.

After working for the doctor for a year, she applied for and got a job with a friend of Dr. Kanzler, a Mr. Bruggmann. He worked as the Swiss minister to the United States. Eventually, with a visa in hand, and a dream in her heart, she made a trip to the United States with Mr. Bruggmann's entourage, where she planned to stay. She met and married Corda Lee Glascow, an American from Austin, Texas where the couple moved permanently. As were many women students in Austria at the time, she had studied at a technical school and became a seamstress. She was able to continue that trade in Texas.

In the early war years there was no bombing in and around the village of Kalsdorf. As the war turned and the Americans and British started bombing raids, Elfie remembers hiding in a tunnel under the streets where pipes traversed or, running to the forest very near the village to hide among the trees. Of course, the hearts of all were pounding and there was terror in the air as they ran for safely. The parents were frantic making sure the children were safe. They could only wish for the safety of the children when they were led to the tunnel under the street. There were basements under the schools but for some reason she does no recall hiding in the school basements.

In late 1944 and early 1945 the town was subjected to more and more bombing as the American and British moved closer. The local target was primarily the factory that produced locks and door handles. The bombers had no idea that they only produced locks and hardware for doors, not weapons. Typical of high altitude bombing the target was frequently missed and the factory was fortunately never hit. Some of the surrounding buildings were hit and destroyed.

Somehow, in a small village, things were quieter and less dangerous for a small child as she continued her schooling. Living in Kalsdorf through the standard schedule of six elementary school grades, she was seven and in second grade as the war was coming to an end. It is difficult to imagine the children calmly walking to school while Hitler's military was advancing, later retreating, on many fronts with military supplies whirling down the roads and streets of Europe. Trains loaded with prisoners were common and the unpredictable orders came from everywhere.

There were a number of Russian prisoners of war housed at the local airport. They were rather loosely supervised, and many were employed in the towns to clean and do manual labor. Elfie was in a position to see some of the prisoners. One saw her and said she looked like his daughter back home and cried at the sight of her. Many of the prisoners spoke German as well as Russian.

And then it was 1945. A small child does not truly take in the chaos and the changes as it fades. The war was over, but the Soviets marched in and took control of eastern Europe including Germany and Austria. The Russian troops were particularly brutal to the civilian population as the officers were unable or unwilling to control their men. Her world was calmer as she started high school in Graz. Elfie started in a private school that was held in a Catholic church. The school required tuition that was paid for by her biological mother who, by this time, had found a job, again as a cook for a doctor Kanzler in a town of Rehetobel, Switzerland.

There were two trains daily into Graz and two return trains in the evening. They had survived the destruction of the war. She had to be very careful to be on time for the train or she would have to walk. In Austria, children were required to go to school until age fifteen or the ninth grade. In high school they could choose an academic track with plans for college or could follow a technical school that lead to a trade school education. Interestingly, one of Elfie's teachers had also taught her mother. In the high school classroom, there were 4 girls sitting on a bench with a long table in front. Their courses included German, English, History, math, and science. One of the teachers taught them how to crochet and cross stitch which they found to be fun.

Many of Elfie's classmates chose the technical rout leading to a trade school education of sewing, and eventually work as tailors or seamstress. Elfie had wanted to be a nanny, taking care of children and did not like the sewing course that so many of the other students liked. The child-care route required a year of home economics followed by three years of childcare.

In her case, Elfie had to wait 6 months for a position to open up at the school, so at age 15 went to Switzerland to work for that period. The school was in Graf, in an attractive building that had been a grand private home in the past. It now functioned as an orphanage with many children whose parents were lost in the war or who were the children of unwed mothers. It had four levels with the office of the school, the kitchen and dining room on the first floor; children's dormitories on the second and third floors; and the students living quarters on the fourth.

Their practical experience involved taking care of the children during the day, making sure they were dressed for the day, that they got to their meals, attended early school time, and had play activities. The students became quite fond of the children thus letting them know they were loved and well cared for. It sounds like a great gift for those children, in contrast to many orphanages across the world where the children were ignored or otherwise poorly cared for. The mothers of many of the children would come for visits once every two weeks. A doctor from town came every two weeks to conducted check-ups on the children.

Our memories are inconsistent as we pass through the stages of our lives. For some reason Elfie does not remember what happened to the children as they got older. Most of the children that they cared for were younger than school age and very few were old enough for school. But she does not remember where the older children would go as they got to school age.

In the evening, the students were provided with classroom lessons and they also did their studies at night. There was not a lot of didactic work, so the studies were not lengthy.

On weekends, students occasionally attended the opera in Graz. The Graz Concert hall had been built in 1885 followed by the opera house in 1899. Those activities seemed to be rather popular with the students. Politically, it was still a chaotic time of post war and its aftermath. Austria was still in an unsettled time with the continued occupation by the Soviet Union. There was talk of a settlement to free up Austria and East Germany but that was in the future.

On completion of the childcare studies the students took a skills test and obtained a certificate in childcare. It was required by the government to have the certificate to get a job taking care of children.

They had a graduation ceremony where all were dressed in their uniforms. These consisted of a long white dress that came almost to the ankles and with long sleeves. There was a white apron with a bib and long front that came down to the bottom of the dress. It was tied with a white sash and bow around the waist. They wore a nurse style cap that was square and was pinned to the hair on the back of their heads. The uniforms were not unlike uniforms worn by nurses in the United States in the early half of the twentieth century

In 1956 the class graduated, and most had job offers in Graz or Vienna waiting for them. The school was well known in Vienna and many families applied to have the students come and work for them as nannies as soon as they graduated. Since Elfie graduated with an excellent mark on her certificate, she would be an ideal candidate for a job. Generally, things were still rather unsettled in the country as Austria had just negotiated independence from the Soviet Union with the help of Great Britain, the United States, and France in 1955. The Russians eventually withdrew their troops but as war reparations, maintained control over the oil in Austria. Compounding the disruption of the time, the Hungarian uprising in late 1955 would involve a great deal of aid from Austria in 1955-56. Receiving and storing the relief supplies was a major issue as plans for this contingency were not well organized. In addition, with Austria's newly gained neutrality they offered humanitarian assistance to Hungarian refugees coming to Austria.

Elfie's first job was in Vienna. Her travels were made difficult because transportation was complicated by the Hungarian issue.

The job included childcare for one child in the family as well as some of the shopping for the household. For those errands she would take the subway to the grocery store where she would do the shopping for the family. It was a task to haul all the groceries home on the subway. There were still a lot of bombed out buildings that had not been rebuild at ten years after the war. The Russians were still a factor as they were moving their troops out slowly.

It was quite exciting for a teenager who was raised in the small village of Kalsdorf to travel to the historic city of Vienna. With the students experience with music and opera during their off time at school, they thought they had moved to heaven in Vienne. There were a lot of tourists in Vienne. It was now ten years after the war and most war damage was cleaned up, but the buildings had not all been repaired. There were a lot of boys from England and Scotland among the tourists who were interested in the girls. They found opportunities to go dancing at clubs and to visit the many parks in the city.

Elfie went to work for an interesting family. The father worked for the state government and was titled as a Barron. The wife's family owned and operated the second largest bakery in Vienna. After two years working for them the wife delivered a second child. Elfie, with the added work, anticipate a raise. That was not what the father was willing to pay. He, however, assisted in getting a new job with a Jewish family by the name of Lichtenstein. They owned an import export business with offices locally and another office in Venezuela. The family included two brothers plus one other partner who switched off running the two offices, so traveled frequently. As a Jewish family the business was a safety valve for family money held in Venezuela and for a potential safe home if anti-Semitism continued after the war.

As one trip was being planned, Elfie was asked if she would like to accompany the family to Venezuela. She therefore spent a year working for the family in Venezuela, an exciting new experience for her. A trip to New York following the trip to Venezuela. Elfie's mother was now in the United States and wanted Elfie to come for a visit. Arrangements were made for Elfie to accompany the Lichtenstein's, stay in New York to sightsee for two weeks followed by a visit to Austin, Texas where her mother was now living. By that time, Elfie had obtained paper for permanent residence and her mother had obtained papers to act as a sponsor.

After her visit to New York, she flew to Fort Worth where she was met by her mother and stepfather, Corder Lee Glasgow. Interesting that she flew to Fort Worth rather than to Austin. It is certainly true that the airport in Austin in the early 1960's was quite small. The terminal building was a wooden structure with no concourses, and one walked out to the airplane to climbed up the stairs to enter the plane.

On arrival in Austin, her mother awakened her early the next morning to ask her to help working on a drapery project. She was a little behind schedule and wanted it finished so that it could be sent on to the customer. The customer was in Seguin, Texas. One must remember that Elfie had chosen childcare over sewing when choosing her school subject as she preferred childcare. There was another factor in place in the U. S. relative to childcare. Dr. Benjamin Spock's book had been published in 1946 and by the early 1960's was still quite popular. It had basically taken over much of the childcare approaches in America, making the recommendations more relaxed than the tradition in Europe and earlier in the United Sates. Elfie realized that this change would be such a departure from her education she would find it a major challenge. She, therefore, continued to work with her mother and the sewing for the time being.

Her mother had a lot of contracts with Scarbroughs, a department store in Austin. Elfie eventually went to work at Scarbroughs where she met some of the other employees. There was another young person whose room mate had recently moved away. She asked Elfie if she would like to rent the other room. Since she had been staying with her mother and did not get along with the stepfather, she thought that would be nice and more independent.

Elfie settled in, continued to work at Scarbroughs and worked with her mother on a number of projects. They had customers locally, but also in Washington, D.C., Florida, Colorado, and California. They even made draperies for the Governor's mansion in Austin. She had some customers who were decorators and for whom she did embroidery and cross stitching. She particularly liked doing the cross stitching.

In her off time, she took classes in adult education at Austin high school including English and history. She found that the teachers at Austin High did not know as much history as she did. She remembered that they did not even know were Lincoln was born. She was very much put off by the level of education taught so eventually quit that school

While living in the new apartment she met the next-door neighbor, Laura Bergstrom, whom she liked very well. Laura had a son whom Elfie met when he offered to help her carry a load of cucumbers to the house. Charles Edward Bergstrom was an Austin native, having been born at Brackenridge Hospital. This was the city hospital and the oldest public hospital west of the Mississippi. He was a dedicated photographer and used those skills in work at Steck Printing. He continued his interest at home with his hobby of photography and built a dark room where he could develop his own pictures. They dated for six months and were married on December 14, 1962 at St Martins Lutheran Church.

They had common interests and definitely the same attitude about money. They didn't buy things if they didn't have cash money to pay for them. Charging items was just not done. They had a friend who had bought a house in north Austin, near Airport Boulevard. Next door to his house was the demonstration house for the new development, and it was now for sale. The price in 1962 was $13,500 with payments of $100 per month including insurance. With both of them working they thought that was in their budget and was about the only thing they bought on time.

Charles built the dark room in the garage. He was quite handy and did all the building of the room. He rewired a small electric organ for St. Martin's Lutheran church to make it functional. He put together equipment to record the sermons from the church so that they could be delivered to member shut-ins at home. He was always repairing toys that belonged to children in the neighborhood. He and Elfie both worked in the garden in their back yard, growing vegetables and flowers. Meanwhile Elfie worked with her mother on many sewing projects with customer all over the country and for

Scarborough's. She does not remember when she retired from that activity. She very much liked to do cross stitching and knitting as she felt she always had to keep her hands busy. She worked that talent into her business.

Elfie never learned to drive well. They had no car in Austria and she never drove during her teenage years or in her several jobs. After they married Charles encouraged her to learn to drive for more independence. She got to the point of taking the driving test but missed one question on the written test, got discouraged, and never completed the requirement for a license. She did get around some on a bicycle.

In 1966 they had a daughter, Anna, for whom she made most of her clothes. Anna eventually attended MacCallum high school in Austin where she played clarinet in the band with the author's son Christopher, and daughter Laura. She is now a teacher in Nixon, Texas and lives in the nearby town of Sequin.

Anna checks on her mother regularly on the week-ends and helps with some of her needs at home. Elfie has quite a lot of arthritis in her knees making a wheelchair or wheeled walker necessary much of the time. She did have a left knee replacement surgery several years ago but that did not help much with her pain while walking.

Then in 2016 Charles died, leaving Elfie living alone in the house they had bought together 54 years earlier. They had been very compatible, thus leaving a huge hole in her life. She has significant difficulty getting around the house and is unable to get out into the back yard to work in the garden. They so liked working together and, of course, she had gardened since childhood. She has wonderful neighbors who come over to help with small chores.

She continues to keep up with Werner, her cousin, after all of these years, making phone calls every few weeks. She considers him a "great guy." He stayed in the home village of Kalsfdorf and worked at the foundry where his father had worked.

Her knees remain her major physical problem for all activities, even with a walker. She never got her driver's license so was without rides to the store and doctor after Charles died. After he died, she became aware of Drive a Senior ATX that provides free transportation and other services to seniors who need help.

Anna supplies her other needs. Drive a Senior, ATX checks on her regularly to make sure she is well supported. She is on the edge of being able to live alone. Her memory is not perfect, so her future is not predictable.

About three months after I had completed our interview, she called our office who notified me that Anna, her daughter, age 58, had died. Anna was significantly overweight and had developed diabetes some years before. She was not taking care of it well recently, according to Elfie, and died of diabetic complications. So, Elfie's major help to living alone is now gone. She has good neighbors but now no family. We have checked with her and she has a will and medical power of attorney and seems to have her affairs in good order. With her neighbors she will get by for a while but, we at Drive a Senior ATX will have to keep close watch to see how she does.

AUTHOR BIOGRAPHY

Christopher S. Chenault, M.D. was born in Los Angeles. He attended Covina California elementary and secondary schools. He got his B.A. at Pomona College in 1960 and his M.D. at Baylor College of Medicine in 1964. He completed a year of internship and eight months of general surgery residency at Harbor General Hospital in Torrance, California before entering the U.S. Public Health Service, Indian Health. He then completed his orthopaedic surgery residency at the University of Iowa Hospitals in 1971. Following his training he entered private practice with the Austin Bone and Joint Clinic in Austin, Texas. Drs. Kermit Fox, Elwood Eichler and Don Greenway and later Bruce Malone, Steven Pearce, and John Pearce provided a nurturing environment for 37 years of practice. For those years he was privileged to have membership on the staffs of Brackenridge, St. David's, Seton, Holy Cross, Seton Northwest and north Austin Medical Center hospitals and serve on a number of committees at those facilities. He is past president of the medical staff at Brackenridge and past president of the Travis County Medical Society. Following "retirement" he has been seeing patients at People's Community Clinic, done some farming, woodworking, photography, writing and playing the guitar. He has been married 60 years and has three children and 8 grandchildren.

He has been on the board of Drive a Senior for 18 years with lots of drives and interactions with clients and their stories.

www.ingramcontent.com/pod-product-compliance
Lightning Source LLC
Chambersburg PA
CBHW020331130626
46549CB00003B/1115